I saw the sweetest flower wild nature yields,
A fresh blown musk-Rose 'twas the first that threw
Its sweets upon the summer ; graceful it grew
As is the wand that Queen Titania wields
And, as I feasted on its fragrancy,
I thought the garden-rose it much excelled.

—KEATS.

THE ROSE ANNUAL 1953

Produced by the Publications Committee of The National Rose Society of Great Britain

---

BERTRAM PARK, O.B.E.
Honorary Editor

CROYDON:
THE CROYDON ADVERTISER LTD.
36, HIGH STREET
1953

TABLE OF CONTENTS

PAGE

ILLUSTRATIONS

COLOURED PLATES

THE NATIONAL ROSE SOCIETY

(*Founded 7th December*, 1876)

Patroness :

HER MOST GRACIOUS MAJESTY QUEEN MARY

Vice-Patrons :

H.R.H. THE PRINCESS ROYAL
THE DUKE AND DUCHESS OF DEVONSHIRE
THE DUKE AND DUCHESS OF PORTLAND
THE DUCHESS OF NORTHUMBERLAND
THE MARQUESS AND MARCHIONESS OF SALISBURY
THE EARL AND COUNTESS OF DERBY

President :

W. E. MOORE

Deputy President :
OLIVER MEE, O.B.E.

Hon. Treasurer :
J. N. HART

Past Presidents :

E. J. BALDWIN
D. L. FLEXMAN
A. E. GRIFFITH
JOHN N. HART
HERBERT OPPENHEIMER
C. C. WILLIAMSON

Vice-Presidents :

L. A. ANSTISS
G. D. BURCH
H. G. CLACY
F. FAIRBROTHER, M.SC.
ALAN GIBBS
W. E. HARKNESS
L. HOLLIS
E. ROYALTON KISCH, M.C.
A. NORMAN
BERTRAM PARK, O.B.E.
L. P. ROBERTS
W. J. W. SANDAY

Council :

M. F. ABBOTT
Miss A. M. ALDOUS
E. M. ALLEN, C.M.G.
K. BENTLEY
A. D. BIDE
R. J. DREW
E. E. GATWARD
C. W. GREGORY
A. B. JOHNSTON
E. B. LE GRICE
H. A. J. MERRYWEATHER
Maj.-Gen. R. F. B. NAYLOR, C.B., D.S.O.
A. E. NEVARD
R. L. PALLETT
S. A. PEARCE
Lieut.-Col. D. POPE
H. ROBINSON
B. W. W. SAMPSON
W. H. SUMPSTER
W. C. THORN
Mrs. C. TISDALL
Mrs. W. T. TOOGOOD
C. F. WARREN
Mrs. A. WHEATCROFT

Regional Representatives :

J. H. ALEXANDER (Scotland)
C. J. DILLON (Northumberland)
ALEX. DICKSON (N. Ireland)
F. FAIRBROTHER, M.SC. (Devon)
W. JOHNSTON (N. Ireland)
J. W. MATTOCK (Oxon)
OLIVER MEE, O.B.E. (Cheshire)
E. H. MORSE (Norfolk)
B. W. PRICE (Gloucester)
W. J. W. SANDAY (Somerset)
A. R. TRESEDER (Wales)
H. WHEATCROFT (Nottinghamshire)

Honorary Vice-Presidents :

Mrs. M. G. CANT
A. L. F. COOK
Rev. GILES DAUBENEY
Dr. G. E. DEACON
E. T. GANN, O.B.E.
J. G. GLASSFORD
Mrs. F. S. HARVEY-CANT
J. HUNTER-SMITH, M.B.E., M.C., B.SC.
Dr. C. LAMPLOUGH
Canon ROLLO MEYER
Dr. W. P. PANCKRIDGE, O.B.E.
J. E. RAYER
W. R. STEINWAY
Dr. H. V. TAYLOR, C.B.E., V.M.H.

Bankers : Messrs. COUTTS & Co., 440, Strand, W.C.

Auditors : BRANNAN, WHITE & CHARLTON, *Chartered Accountants*, 23, Lawrence Lane, Cheapside, E.C.2

Hon. Editor : BERTRAM PARK, O.B.E. **Secretary :** H. EDLAND

117, Victoria Street, Westminster, S.W.1 (P.O. Box 84)

Telephone : VICtoria 0959 *Telegrams* : Natiorose, Sowest, London

STANDING COMMITTEES FOR 1953

Finance and General Purposes Committee:

G. D. BURCH	L. HOLLIS	W. J. W. SANDAY
F. FAIRBROTHER	E. ROYALTON KISCH	W. H. SUMPSTER
W. E. HARKNESS	A. NORMAN	H. WHEATCROFT
	L. P. ROBERTS	

Trial Ground Committee:

G. D. BURCH	E. ROYALTON KISCH	Maj.-Gen. R. F. B. NAYLOR
C. W. GREGORY	E. B. LE GRICE	A. NORMAN
W. E. HARKNESS	J. W. MATTOCK	H. WHEATCROFT
	E. H. MORSE	

Co-opted:

R. LINE, B.Sc., A. H. LUGG, N.D.H., Herts Institute of Agriculture.

Publications Committee:

Miss A. M. ALDOUS	L. HOLLIS	A. NORMAN
A. D. BIDE	E. ROYALTON KISCH	L. P. ROBERTS
G. D. BURCH	E. B. LE GRICE	Mrs. A. WHEATCROFT
	H. A. J. MERRYWEATHER	

Exhibitions Committee:

G. D. BURCH	ALAN GIBBS	J. W. MATTOCK
H. G. CLACY	W. E. HARKNESS	A. NORMAN
F. FAIRBROTHER	L. HOLLIS	Mrs. C. TISDALL
	E. ROYALTON KISCH	

The Officers, Past Presidents, the Chairman of each Committee and Hon. Editor are ex-officio members of all Standing Committees.

ARRANGEMENTS, 1953

The Exhibitions.—The Summer Show is to be held in the Royal Horticultural Society's Halls, Westminster, on the 3rd and 4th July next. On the first day in both Halls, and in the New Hall only on the second day. The Provincial Show at Vivary Park, Taunton, on Thursday and Friday, 6th and 7th August, and the Autumn Show in both Horticultural Halls, Westminster, on the 18th September.

Schedules for these Shows will be forwarded to members **on application.** All interested are cordially invited to apply to the Secretary.

Admission Tickets.—The number of tickets to which each member is entitled in 1953 remains the same as last year, and is :—

To One Guinea Subscribers :

A Membership Card admitting holder to the Society's Shows in London, and to several other Provincial Shows held under the auspices of local Societies ; five transferable tickets for the Summer Show, and three transferable tickets for the Autumn Show.

To Half-Guinea Subscribers :

A Membership Card similar to that received by the One Guinea subscriber ; one transferable ticket for the Summer Show and one transferable ticket for the Autumn Show.

Extra Tickets.—Members may purchase from the Society's offices extra tickets for the Summer and Autumn Shows at reduced rates : 5/- tickets for 3/6, and 2/6 tickets for 1/6. The prices of public admission to the Shows will be : Summer Show, first day 5/-, second day 2/6 ; the Autumn Show 2/6.

N.R.S. Classes at Provincial Shows.—By the courtesy of the Organisers, special classes for members of the National Rose Society are offered in 1953 at the undermentioned Shows :—

Edinburgh, September 2nd, 3rd and 4th. Secretary : Mr. Maurice G. Kidd, 13, Melville Street, Edinburgh, 3.

Formby, July 4th. Secretary : S. E. Lytle, Northcote, 76, Raven Meols Lane, Formby.

Newcastle-upon-Tyne, August 7th and 8th. Hon. Secretary : Mr. S. Carson, 77, Strathmore Road, Gosforth, Newcastle-upon-Tyne, 3.

Nottingham, St. Ann's Rose Show, July 11th and 12th. Secretary : Mr. J. E. Icke, 29, Sketchley Street, Blue Bell Hill Road, Nottingham.

Southport, August 26th, 27th and 28th. Flower Show Secretary: Mr. G. W. Nicholls, Victoria Buildings, Lord Street, Southport.

Swansea (The Magnet Club), August 22nd. Hon. Secretary : Mr. W. J. Hopkins, Engineering Department, Ravenhill Works, Fforestfach, Swansea.

Schedules of any of these Shows can be obtained on application to the respective Secretaries.

Admission to Provincial Shows.—Arrangements have also been made again this year whereby the Society's Membership Card will admit the holder free of charge to the following Shows :—

Bristol and District Group of N.R.S. Members' Show at The Corn Exchange, Bristol, on July 8th, 11.30 a.m. to 7.30 p.m.

Formby Horticultural and Agricultural Society's Show at The Park, Duke Street, Formby, on July 4th, 10 a.m. to 7.30 p.m.

Hitchin Horticultural Society's Show at Butt's Close, Hitchin, on June 27th, 1 p.m. to 8 p.m.

Ipswich and East of England Horticultural Society's Show at Christchurch Park, Ipswich, on July 15th, 2.15 p.m. to 8 p.m.

North of England Rose, Carnation and Sweet Pea Society's Show at Exhibition Park, Newcastle-upon-Tyne, on August 7th and 8th, 1.30 p.m. to 9.30 p.m. and 10 a.m. to 7 p.m.

Nottingham Garden Holders' Association, St. Ann's Rose Society's Show at The Arboretum, Nottingham, on July 11th and 12th, 3 p.m. to 9.30 p.m. and 10 a.m. to 9 p.m.

Royal Caledonian Horticultural Society's Show, Waverley Market, Edinburgh, on September 2nd, 3rd and 4th, 12 noon to 9 p.m., 10 a.m. to 9 p.m. and 10 a.m. to 6 p.m.

The Magnet Club Horticultural Society's Show at Ravenhill Garage, Swansea, on August 22nd, 12 noon to 7 p.m.

The Council again acknowledges with grateful thanks the generous co-operation of all Societies concerned in the foregoing arrangements. The N.R.S. Membership Card will admit the holder only, but accompanying visitors can gain admission by payment at entrance. New members and exhibitors will be cordially welcomed by the various Societies.

Information Bureaux.—Arrangements are being completed for Information Bureaux at The Chelsea Show (May 20th, 21st and 22nd) and the "Evening News" Show, Olympia (date not fixed at time of printing), in addition to the Society's own Shows. Visits from members are cordially invited.

The Trial Ground.—The Trial Ground is situated in The Institute of Agriculture, Oaklands, St. Albans, and will be open to members in 1953 on the following dates :—

VISITING DAYS

Saturdays— June 27th, July 11th, 25th, August 8th, 22nd, September 5th, 19th.

Wednesdays— July 1st, 15th, 29th, August 12th, 26th, September 9th and 23rd.

Members are requested to comply with the following simple rules made for visits during 1953.

RULES FOR VISITORS

1.—Admission shall be restricted to members on production of the current Membership Card, which will admit the holder and one friend **on the dates specified above only, between the hours of 10 a.m. and 5 p.m.**

2.—Members shall be required to sign the Visitors' Book.

3.—Rose blooms, buds, trees or parts of trees must not in any circumstances be taken from the Trial Ground.

Lantern Slides, Library.—Full particulars of the above privileges of membership will gladly be sent to members on application to the Secretary.

Identification of Rose Blooms.—Members seeking to identify varieties, the names of which are unknown to them, are asked to write to the expert nearest to their locality (see page 12), and if possible more than one bloom of each variety should be sent—the ideal number is three showing the different stages of development, the bud, the half-open bloom and the three-parts open bloom. Some wood and foliage would also help, together with a brief description of the habit and approximate age of the variety. If the blooms are placed in water for at least six hours before despatch, they are less likely to drop during transit.

A stamped addressed envelope for reply should be enclosed with the blooms.

W. K. BENTLEY, c/o Walter Bentley and Sons, Rose Nurseries, Loughborough Road, Wanlip, Leics.

D. BIDE, c/o S. Bide and Sons, Alma Nurseries, Farnham, Surrey.

C. J. DILLON, Springfield Nurseries, Woolsington, Kenton, Newcastle-upon-Tyne.

HENRY DREW, Rose Grower, Longworth, Abingdon, Berks.

C. W. GREGORY, c/o C. Gregory and Son Ltd., Chilwell, Nottingham.

W. E. HARKNESS, c/o R. Harkness and Co., The Rose Gardens, Hitchin, Herts.

E. B. LE GRICE, Roseland Nurseries, North Walsham, Norfolk.

A. E. NEVARD, c/o B. R. Cant and Sons Ltd., Old Rose Gardens, Colchester, Essex.

H. A. J. MERRYWEATHER, c/o H. Merryweather and Sons Ltd., Southwell, Notts.

E. H. MORSE, c/o Henry Morse and Sons, Westfield Nurseries, Brundall, Norwich.

R. V. ROGER, The Nurseries, Pickering, N. Yorks.

E. W. STEDMAN, c/o E. W. Stedman Ltd., The Rose Gardens, Peterborough.

A. R. TRESEDER, c/o Stephen Treseder and Son, Ely Nurseries, Ely, Cardiff.

A. and H. WHEATCROFT, c/o Wheatcroft Bros. Ltd., Ruddington, Nottingham.

Extra Copies of Publications.—Members may purchase extra copies post free of " The Rose Annual for 1953," price 8/6, the new edition of " Roses: A Select List and Guide to Pruning," price 5/-, " The Enemies of the Rose," price 7/6, and " Hints on Planting Roses," price 1/-, on application to the Secretary.

Subscriptions and Resignations.—Members are reminded that subscriptions are due and payable on 1st January in each year. Any member wishing to resign must give notice to the Secretary on or before 1st February, after which date the member will be liable for the subscription for the current year.

H. EDLAND,
Secretary.

NATIONAL ROSE SOCIETY,
117, Victoria Street, London, S.W.1.

REPORT OF THE COUNCIL FOR YEAR ENDED 31st DECEMBER, 1952

The Council is gratified to report that all previous records of new enrolments were broken in 1952, no fewer than 8,242 new members being obtained. This brings the total membership to 32,500 after allowing for some 3,200 losses from deaths and resignations. The Council is conscious of the fact that this achievement has been possible only through a concerted effort, and therefore expresses to all members its grateful thanks.

THE SOCIETY'S STATUS

The Inland Revenue has recognised the Society as a body of persons established for charitable purposes on the ground that the Society's main object is of benefit to the community. This has resulted in a refund of Income Tax on the invested funds of the Society as from April, 1949. Although further tax could be recovered by covenanted subscriptions the Council has decided not to pursue the matter.

FINANCE

The Revenue Account for the year shows an excess of Revenue over Expenditure of £2,467, and the Reserve for new publications now stands at £700. The object of this Reserve is to spread the high cost of new editions of the Society's handbooks over the years during which the need for them accrues, in order to avoid a very heavy burden falling on the actual year of publication.

Repayments of Income Tax on income from investments, etc., for the back period from 6th April, 1949, to 31st December, 1951, have been credited direct to the Surplus Account, as shown in the Balance Sheet, and the amount repayable for 1952 (£339) is included in the Revenue Account.

Partly because of the altered status of the Society, referred to above, certain changes have been made in the investments during the year. Amounts standing to the Society's credit with the Post Office Savings Bank and the Alliance Building Society, aggregating £5,442, were withdrawn and £5,375 was invested in 4 per cent. Consolidated Stock, to which further amounts totalling £4,500 were added later in the year.

PUBLICATIONS

In April, 1952, the Rose Annual was distributed to all members. The number of letters received showed that members were highly appreciative of the efforts of those who so kindly contributed to and helped in its compilation.

In early August the new edition of "Roses: a Select List and Guide to Pruning" was distributed to those members from whom applications had been received. The total number issued was 14,000, which represented a saving of approximately fifty per cent., the membership at that date being approximately 28,000. As the cost of publications absorbs such a large proportion of a member's subscription the amount saved by this procedure is available for the extension of the Society's aims, and also helps the Society to retain its minimum subscription of 10s. 6d. per annum. It is pointed out, however, that any member who has not received a copy can still make an application.

TRIAL GROUND

The Trial Ground at St. Albans continues to be well supported by hybridists throughout the world, no fewer than 140 new bush varieties and 57 climbing varieties being sent for trial in 1952. The trees did well, coming into bloom earlier than last year. If the Rules governing the conditions under which varieties are accepted for trial had been strictly observed, a large number of trees which had completed their trials would have been taken out, but the Council retained many varieties in view of the great interest taken by visitors. It has now been agreed that the trials shall be extended from two years to three years, and this will ensure a reasonable number of trees always being in the Trial Ground for inspection. In future all trees which have completed their trials will be lifted in accordance with the new ruling. The extension of visiting hours enabled a record number of visitors to examine the varieties and view the ground.

SHOWS

The Summer Show was held in the Royal Horticultural Society's Halls on the 27th and 28th June, in both Halls on the first day and in the New Hall only on the second day. This extension of the Show proved as popular as in 1951 when it was in the nature of an experiment : the probability is that it will now be a permanent feature. The blooms displayed reached a very high standard, and the Show attracted a very large attendance. It has been decided to open future Shows an hour earlier, namely at 11 a.m. instead of 12 noon, and this should assist in affording members greater ease in which to view the exhibits. The Provincial Show was held at Manchester in conjunction with the Manchester Flower Show on July 25th and 26th. The weather prior to Show week had not been good but was excellent throughout the Show, which, judging from comments made by visitors, was thoroughly enjoyed by all who attended. The Council expresses appreciation of the kindliness and wholehearted co-operation of the Manchester Flower Show Committee which contributed so much to the success of the venture. The Autumn Show was held in both of the R.H.S. Halls on September 19th. In size the Show was a record, but unfortunately the weather was very trying and many blooms were showing the effect of it. Most visitors, however, were agreeably surprised at their quality. It may be that members of the Council tend to become hypercritical, expecting every Show to be better than the previous one !

The organisers of various other leading Shows throughout the Country again included classes reserved for members of the National Rose Society, and granted free admission to the Shows on production of the Member's card. The Council tenders thanks to the various organisers for these concessions which were much appreciated by members.

INFORMATION AND ADVICE BUREAUX

Bureaux were established at the three Exhibitions of the Society ; also at Bristol, Chelsea and the " Evening News " Show, and owing to their popularity and usefulness similar arrangements are in hand for 1953.

ADVICE TO MEMBERS : LIBRARY : LANTERN SLIDES : LECTURES

A record number of enquiries have been dealt with during the past year. This is very gratifying and is an indication of the interest in our National Flower.

The difficulty of identifying Rose blooms will be appreciated, and to spread this work over as wide a field as possible members are particularly requested to read details of this special service on page 11 of the Rose Annual.

The demand for library books in past years has been heavy, but the added membership resulted in greater use being made of the books than ever before. Unfortunately many of them are now out of print, which prevents the replacement of those badly worn, and the Council would ask the indulgence of members for the condition of these. At the same time it might be mentioned the Council would appreciate any gifts of books on the Rose to add to the library.

The lantern slides continue to prove of interest and there is a constant demand for illustrated lectures.

DEAN HOLE MEMORIAL MEDAL AWARDS

The Council has awarded the Dean Hole Memorial Medal to the retiring President and to Mr. Bertram Park who has made valuable contributions to our cause over a number of years and more recently as Honorary Editor.

Likewise it gives the Council great pleasure to announce that this coveted award has been made to Dr. A. S. Thomas, President of The National Rose Society of Victoria. He has held office with distinction since 1938, but for a break in 1949 and 1950, and has given outstanding service in the interests of Rose culture throughout Australia and New Zealand. Dr. Thomas will be visiting this country during 1953 when we shall have the great pleasure of presenting the medal.

OBITUARY

The Council has, with very great regret, to record the death of Mr. A. Norman Rogers, a Past President and for many years the Society's Honorary Treasurer ; also of Mr. A. J. Macself, an old member of the Society and a regular contributor to the Rose Annual.

CONCLUSION

In conclusion the Council again expresses thanks to all members for the support afforded in various ways and for the record enrolment of new members.

By Order of the Council,

D. L. Flexman, *President.*

THE HON. TREASURER, ON BEHALF OF THE COUNCIL, WOULD LIKE TO EXPRESS APPRECIATION OF THE ADDITIONAL FINANCIAL ASSISTANCE AFFORDED BY THOSE MEMBERS WHO KINDLY SENT HIM THE HIGHER SUBSCRIPTION OF TWENTY-ONE SHILLINGS

REVENUE ACCOUNT FOR THE YEAR ENDED 31st DECEMBER, 1952

1951 £	£		£	£	£
		PUBLICATIONS			
6,941		Expenditure		8,661	
+1,000		*Less* Charged against Reserve for New Editions		800	
7,941				7.861	
150		*Less* Sales	137		
737		Advertising Revenue	722		
				859	
	7,054				7.002
		SHOWS			
1,575		Prize Monies, Medals and Plate ...		1,421	
549		Expenses		622	
2,124				2,043	
573		*Less* Proceeds		655	
	1,551				1.388
		TRIAL GROUND			
	680	Expenditure			713
		SECRETARIAL & OFFICE EXPENSES			
2,388		Salaries, Pensions and Assistance		2,904	
561		Rent, etc.		577	
515		Printing and Stationery		768	
1,334		Postages, Telephone, Hire of Rooms, etc.		1,742	
35		Repairs and Renewals		66	
74		Auditors' Fees		73	
	4,907				6.130
	676	ADVERTISING & PUBLICITY ...			1,012
		DONATION			
	26	International Horticultural Congress			—
	313	INCOME TAX			—
	15,207				16.245
		BALANCE			
	638	Excess of Revenue over Expenditure for the year			2,467
	15,845				18.712

1951 £		£	£
	SUBSCRIPTIONS & AFFILIATION FEES		
14,849	Subscriptions	17.474	
246	Affiliation Fees	327	
			17.801
15,095			
	INCOME FROM INVESTMENTS, ETC.		
745	Gross		911
	PREMIUM ON REDEMPTION		
5	3% Defence Bonds		—
15,845			18.712

BALANCE SHEET, 31st DECEMBER, 1952

1951 £		£	£
	SURPLUS:—		
	Balance 1st January, 1952	23,294	
	Add Income Tax Recovered—6th April, 1949, to 31st December, 1951	824	
	Excess of Revenue over Expenditure for the year ended 31st December, 1952	2,467	
23,294			26,585
	RESERVE FOR NEW EDITIONS OF PUBLICATIONS		
	Balance 1st January, 1952	1,500	
	Less Expended during the year	800	
1,500			700
	CURRENT LIABILITIES:—		
266	Sundry Creditors	2,525	
3,265	Subscriptions received in advance (excluding Life Members)	4,220	
			6,745
£28,325			£34,030

AUDITORS' REPORT

To the Members, National Rose Society

We have audited the above Balance Sheet, dated 31st December, 1952, and the Revenue Account for the year ended on that date and have obtained all the information and explanations we have required. In our opinion such Balance Sheet and Revenue Account are properly drawn up so as to exhibit a true and correct view of the Society's affairs according to the best of our information and explanations given to us and as shown by the books of the Society. We have verified the Securities representing the Investments of your Society at 31st December, 1952, and have found the same to be in order.

BRANNAN, WHITE AND CHARLTON,
Chartered Accountants, Auditors.

23, Lawrence Lane,
LONDON, E.C.2.
8th January, 1953.

1951 £		£	£
	FIXED ASSETS:—		
2,028	FREEHOLD HOUSE: 23, Orchard Close, St Albans, at cost		2,028
	OFFICE FURNITURE, ETC.		
50	Balance 1st January, 1952		50
125	LIBRARY as valued by the Secretary ..		125
2,203			2,203
	INVESTMENTS at Cost:—		
	£3,400 Conversion Stock 3½% 1961 or after	2,582	
	£4,887 18s. 9d. British Transport 3% Guaranteed Stock 1978/88	3,617	
	£1,500 Mersey Docks and Harbour Board 3¼% Deb. Stock 1970/80	1,084	
	£300 Met. Water "B" 3% Stock	195	
	£2,000 2½% Defence Bonds	2,000	
	£1,000 Savings Bonds 3% 1955/65	1,000	
	£2,000 Savings Bonds 3% 1960/70	1,968	
	£3,486 1s. 6d. Savings Bonds 2½% 1964/67 ..	3,547	
	£500 2½% National War Bonds "A"	500	
	£12,548 2s. 5d. 4% Consolidated Stock ..	11,270	
20,965			27,763
(20,455)	**Market Value 31st December, 1952 .. £27,016**		
	INVESTMENTS PRESENTED TO THE SOCIETY (not valued):—		
	27 New England Electric System Common Shares		
	5 Louisiana Power and Light Co. Pref. Shares		
	5 Standard Gas and Electric Light Co. Prior Pref. Shares		
	CURRENT ASSETS:—		
1,054	STOCK OF PUBLICATIONS as valued by the Secretary	2,114	
4,103	CASH AT BANKERS ON DEPOSIT AND CURRENT ACCOUNT AND IN HAND	1,729	
—	INCOME TAX RECOVERABLE	221	4,064
£28,325			£34,030

PRESIDENTS OF THE NATIONAL ROSE SOCIETY

1877–1904	The Very Rev. DEAN HOLE, V.M.H.
1905–06	CHARLES E. SHEA.
1907–08	E. B. LINDSELL.
1909–10	Rev. F. PAGE-ROBERTS.
1911–12	Rev. J. H. PEMBERTON.
1913–14	CHARLES E. SHEA.
1915–16	EDWARD MAWLEY, V.M.H.
1917–18	Sir EDWARD HOLLAND.
1919–20	H. R. DARLINGTON, V.M.H.
1921–22	Sir EDWARD HOLLAND.
1923–24	SYDNEY F. JACKSON.
1925–26	C. C. WILLIAMSON.
1927–28	H. R. DARLINGTON, V.M.H.
1929–30	ARTHUR JOHNSON.
1931–32	HERBERT OPPENHEIMER.
1933–34	Dr. A. H. WILLIAMS.
1935–36	Major A. D. G. SHELLEY, R.E.
1937–38	HERBERT OPPENHEIMER.
1939–40	JOHN N. HART.
1941–42	CHARLES H. RIGG.
1943–44	HERBERT OPPENHEIMER.
1945–46	A. NORMAN ROGERS.
1947–48	A. E. GRIFFITH.
1949–50	E. J. BALDWIN.
1951–52	D. L. FLEXMAN.
1953	WILLIAM E. MOORE.

DEAN HOLE MEDALLISTS

1909	Rev. J. H. PEMBERTON.
1910	EDWARD MAWLEY, V.M.H.
1912	GEORGE DICKSON, V.M.H.
1914	CHARLES E. SHEA.
1917	E. B. LINDSELL.
1918	Sir EDWARD HOLLAND.
1919	Rev. F. PAGE-ROBERTS.
1919	GEORGE PAUL.
1920	H. R. DARLINGTON, V.M.H.
1921	S. McGREDY.
1923	Miss E. WILLMOTT, F.L.S.
1924	SYDNEY F. JACKSON.
1925	COURTNEY PAGE.
1926	C. C. WILLIAMSON.
1930	Dr. J. CAMPBELL HALL.
1930	WILLIAM E. NICKERSON.
1931	ARTHUR JOHNSON.
1933	HERBERT OPPENHEIMER.
1935	Dr. A. H. WILLIAMS.
1935	WALTER EASLEA.
1936	ALISTER CLARK.
1937	Major A. D. G. SHELLEY, R.E.
1940	JOHN N. HART.
1942	CHARLES H. RIGG.
1942	Dr. HORACE J. McFARLAND.
1945	Dr. H. V. TAYLOR, O.B.E.
1947	A. NORMAN ROGERS.
1948	Dr. G. E. DEACON.
1949	W. E. MOORE.
1949	A. E. GRIFFITH.
1950	JOHN RAMSBOTTOM, O.B.E., Dr.Sc., M.A.
1950	F. S. HARVEY-CANT, M.B.E. (Posthumously).
1951	E. J. BALDWIN.
1952	D. L. FLEXMAN.
1952	BERTRAM PARK, O.B.E.
1952	Dr. A. S. THOMAS.

[*Arranged by Constance Spry, Ltd.*

THE BOWL OF ROSES

Presented to Her Majesty Queen Mary by the members of the National Rose Society on the occasion of Her Majesty's birthday, 1952.

MARLBOROUGH HOUSE
S.W.1.

29th May, 1952.

Dear Sir,

I have received Queen Mary's commands to write and thank you most warmly for two charming gifts from the National Rose Society on the anniversary of her Birthday.

Her Majesty is enchanted with the vase of really lovely roses and says that they are a real joy to her in her sitting room. Queen Mary is also most grateful for the copy of The Rose Annual for this year in its beautiful binding.

Her Majesty hopes that you will be able to let the members of the National Rose Society know how greatly she values their kind thoughts of her on her Birthday again this year and their lovely presents.

Yours very truly,

[signature]

Private Secretary to H.M. Queen Mary

D.L. Flexman, Esq.,
President
The National Rose Society.

"SEVENTY-FIVE YEARS"

D. L. FLEXMAN

"THE Amateur Rose grower has made as much progress as George III with his fiddle." Yes, it was S. Reynolds Hole born in 1819, the only son of S. Hole, Squire of Caunton in Nottinghamshire, who said that, when he was Dean of Rochester. But perhaps we are travelling too fast for the reader, for even a Dean has to make a start, and it was as Curate of Caunton in 1844.

Between 1850 and 1887 when he was Vicar of Caunton he promoted and arranged the first "Grand National Rose Show" in St. James's Hall. To be precise it was in 1858. What a lover of the Rose he must have been ; it is recorded that at this period he was growing 400 varieties ! I do not know, but I doubt if there was another Amateur in the country growing 400 varieties, nor can I think of one to-day.

To write of the life of Dean Hole is to write about Roses and the National Rose Society. Conversely one cannot write of the N.R.S. without writing of the Dean because it was his ability, knowledge and zeal that were responsible for the formation of the Society in 1876. It is so often said that Dean Hole was the founder of the Society that it is incumbent upon me at this juncture to introduce the Reverend H. Honeywood D'ombrain, V.M.H., for it was he who founded the Society and became and remained for 25 years its Honorary Secretary.

Reynolds Hole—he was appointed Dean of Rochester in 1887—was the first President, a position he retained from 1877-1904.

In 1878 Edward Mawley was appointed co-Secretary. He, too, was one of the band of enthusiastic Rosarians who attended the first meeting of the N.R.S.

Mr. D'ombrain described the foundation in the following words : "It was a murky December day in 1876 that the most representative gathering of Rosarians ever held in this country met together in the rooms of the Horticultural Club on the Adelphi Terrace to consider what could be done to advance the interest of the Rose, for in truth the Queen of Flowers had fallen on evil days. Two-day Shows were the rule rather than the exception ; there was no real classification of exhibitors, or indeed of exhibits ; the French plan seemed to have come into vogue, namely, that of classes for a large number of flowers without much reference to their character. Summer Roses were largely in evidence on Exhibition stands, and quantity, not quality, appeared to be the object aimed at by Societies."

This criticism obviously related to the Rose Shows held in the two decades preceding the formation of the National Rose Society, namely, the " Grand National Rose Shows " which the Dean promoted. " Grand National " here affords me an opportunity of reminding readers that he was a fearless rider to hounds, a fine preacher, scholar and all-round sportsman.

The founders appear to have decided to limit the Shows—and showing seems to have been foremost in their minds—to one day affairs and not to two or three as in the past, as no bloom can be at its best on two days, especially under canvas ! It was not until 1925 that a two-day Summer Show was again introduced. A one day Show is preferable for the Amateur because while the Trade can furbish up for the second day (at the expense of budding eyes !) the Amateur exhibits are usually blown or wilted. It is interesting to note Mr. Darlington's observations at that time on two-day Shows, especially the condition of the blooms on the second day.

> " This is a considerable achievement due in part to the advance in the merits of the Rose, and in part to that of the skill and taste of exhibitors ; and so far as it leads to the selection of young and fresh flowers, and the rejection of over blown and fading blooms it is all to the good."

Only in 1951 were two-day Shows resumed after a lapse of eleven years, and that extension was restricted to Trade exhibits, the Amateur exhibits being cleared after the first day.

At the first meeting Canon Hole accepted the presidency, the Rev. H. Honeywood D'ombrain was nominated as Secretary and Mr. Horace K. Mayor as Treasurer, and it was decided to hold an exhibition at St. James's Hall, the largest one then available. It appears to have been a grand Show except in the sense that financially it was a complete failure. The prize winners consented to take a portion of their money, and with the position thus eased, the founders decided to forge ahead and wait for better times to recover their loss. The " Cranston " Cup (50 guineas) for Amateurs was won by Mr. T. Jowett, of Hereford, with a box of 48 while the 36 and 24 were won respectively by Mr. R. G. N. Baker, of Exeter, and Mr. J. Atkinson, of Brentwood.

At this juncture it would not be inappropriate to record the Dean's advice to Amateur exhibitors. Wherever possible he favoured cutting on the morning of the Show. "At 3.30 you should be among your Roses."

In the Nurserymen's classes Paul and Sons, of Cheshunt, were first for 72 distinct varieties, the 48 singles and 24 trebles going to Messrs. Cranston, of Hereford.

Boxes were then the order of the day, but the reporter wrote : " It was impossible to make any artistic arrangement, but Messrs. Veitch and Son, of Chelsea, and Messrs. Laing and Co., of Forest Hill, kindly contributed plants for the centre line of tables, so breaking the dead level ; but all experience tends to show that nothing can supersede the present style of boxes—and that being the case, all idea of artistic arrangement must be abandoned."

It was the day of the Hybrid Perpetual with a few Teas, presumably to emphasize the gargantuan proportions of the former. The only Hybrid Tea then recognized as such was " Cheshunt Hybrid."

There are, fortunately, even to-day, judges who prize quality and form before size ; to quote Darlington, " In which all beauty of form has been lost in a mere mass of bloated vegetation."

From St. James's Hall to the Crystal Palace in 1878, Temple Gardens in 1901, Royal Botanic Society's Gardens, Regent's Park, in 1905, Chelsea in 1927 and the Royal Horticultural Society's Halls in Vincent Square where the Shows are still staged—the two halls being required to accommodate an increasing number of exhibitors—is the order of progression. In 1925 the Summer Show attracted no fewer than 3,500 visitors.

To-day with a membership of over 30,000 the schedules of the Society provide for large trade groups which are a great attraction, decorative classes to interest the ladies (introduced in 1899), Roses in bowls, baskets, vases and boxes, catering for those who grow a thousand or more plants to novices with their dozens soon to develop into the 250 or 500 classification.

The classes for Roses in vases were introduced during the period when the Metropolitan Shows were held in the Temple Gardens 1901-1904. Another landmark was when in 1904 on the suggestion of Messrs. E. J. Holland, Courtney Page and Frank Cant the Society decided to hold an Autumn Show, the first being held in the R.H.S. Hall, Vincent Square. Baskets seem to have been introduced in 1910 and I find Mr. Darlington commenting on the fact that they possess one disadvantage to the Amateur in that the flowers have to be cut with long stems 15 to 18 inches in length, somewhat seriously weakening their plants. Prior to 1892 the schedules were very open but in that year a Mr. C. T. Grahame suggested a plan by which exhibitors were classed in sections determined by the number of plants grown. A sub-division of exhibitors has persisted to the present day, thus amply justifying what was then an innovation.

The objects of the National Rose Society, according to the Constitution and Rules, are to disseminate knowledge of the Rose and Rose growing and to encourage, improve and extend the cultivation of the Rose by means of scientific trials, the holding of exhibitions, publications and other activities. These have been the Society's objects since the day of its formation. Has that object been achieved? From 1878 to 1900 the membership slowly increased to something over 500. By 1910 it had nearly doubled itself during the previous four years and stood at 3,797 : three times that of 1904. History is repeating itself for our membership has practically doubled itself in the past four years, but instead of being just under 4,000, as it was in 1910, it is now over 30,000. All these and others who have not yet joined our ranks derive great benefit from the exhibitions, scientific trials, lectures and the thousands of pounds expended on the production and distribution of Rose literature. In short the work of the Council, entirely voluntary and unpaid, makes an invaluable contribution to mental and physical well-being. The answer therefore to the question I posed at the beginning of this paragraph is indubitably, yes.

Nothing so far has been said about the showing of Roses grown under glass. Inaugurated in 1913 by the holding of a Spring Show, the austere conditions of the past decade compelled their suspension, but the Society's publications have dealt very fully with this aspect of Rose growing. Provincial Shows, too, had to be suspended but have been revived. 1950 Wolverhampton, 1951 Stratford-upon-Avon, 1952 Manchester. It is, therefore, of especial interest to recall that our first Provincial Show was held in 1880 at Manchester, then famous for its excellent exhibitions.

To encourage the raising of new Roses the Society in 1883 instituted its Gold Medal and it has been a much coveted award ever since. The first went in 1883 to the Rose " Her Majesty," and the second was awarded in 1885 to " Mrs. John Laing." Until quite recently it was necessary for the raiser or exhibitor of a new variety to stage not only blooms, but a complete plant so that the habit of growth could be considered, but now that the new Trial Ground has been established at St. Albans no Rose will be considered for a Gold Medal unless it is or has been under trial in these grounds. No matter how beautiful are the blooms exhibited at the Show a Gold Medal is not now awarded unless the trials show that the plants have been of good report, and a panel of experienced judges, representing both the trade and the amateur, determines this.

Members of the Society are assured, therefore, as far as it is humanly possible, that such a Rose will, with good cultivation, live up to its award.

The Trial Ground was started at Haywards Heath in 1928 adjacent to the residence of the late Honorary Secretary, Mr. Courtney Page. On his death it was transferred to St. Albans where the conditions are admirably suited to these trials and the position not inaccessible.

Members only are allowed to visit the Ground on specified days, at specified times, and in addition are required to sign the Visitors' Book. The rules regarding these visits must of necessity be restrictive as supervision of visitors is required—and there is work to be done !

The invitation to contribute this article to the Annual affords me a suitable opportunity to pay further tributes to the work of the late Mr. Courtney Page, our Honorary Secretary from 1915-1947 ; a past President, the late Mr. H. R. Darlington, V.M.H., who over a lifetime contributed so much to our Society in general and the Annual in particular—without which these notes could never have been penned—and to the late Mr. Sydney Harvey-Cant, for whom I had a great affection, and who, with our late Honorary Secretary in 1932, was responsible for the formation of the Association of British Rose Producers. It is to these and other friends, who shall be nameless, that a great part of my life has been cast in happy places.

These notes will not be complete without reference to Her Most Gracious Majesty Queen Mary, our Patroness, who consented to occupy the vacant place and to become Patroness of the Society in succession to Queen Alexandra.

WE TALK ABOUT SUCH THINGS

W. J. W. SANDAY, Bristol

It is good occasionally to get away from technicalities and somewhat sombre writings down to a chat and the things that are everyday talk among friends growing and showing Roses. One such friend came to me at the Autumn Show to say that following persistent effort for several years he had at last secured his first prize card. He could not have looked more pleased if someone had told him of a big win in some sweepstake and I warrant that if you asked him he would say it was the best thing that happened in 1952. Certainly nothing will ever pull him away from Roses.

At the same Show a well known and respected member of the Trade, looking tired after spending most of the night staging, wondered if he was too old for this " show business " and then rather whimsically said, " but I suppose I shall be doing it all over again next year ! " Of course he will because Rose growing is not just a living to the Nurseryman, it is fundamentally his life's work and hobby rolled into one, a desire to produce the best and within it all the same competitive spirit possessed by the amateur. Nothing short of calamity can stop us showing when once the " bug " has bitten. Remember dear old Gulliver Speight—he went on until it was difficult for him to distinguish the colours in his box and with the same old scissors on a piece of string around his waist.

Of course there will be a time when all your good flowers pass their best the day before the Show—it happens to us all. There is really only one sensible bit of advice and that is to grow more Roses, but in any case be heartened by the old saying " every dog has his day," and it's only a matter of trying all the time.

Someone rang me up the other day and asked if decorative Roses to be arranged in bowls and vases would carry a hundred miles out of water and how did I suggest it should be done. Blooms cut in the late afternoon and left in water for a few hours will certainly carry out of water packed in boxes without fear, particularly in the Autumn, and it is probably the best way to avoid bruising. If you do decide to carry in a water container see the blooms are as close together as possible to avoid movement and in any event with either method put wool ties around all blooms likely to " blow."

What about box blooms that have been tied on the trees a day or two before the Show? It is wise to remove the ties to see if the bloom is " holding " after which re-tie, put the bloom in the box and leave the dressing until the journey is over and the box on the Show Bench.

In disbudding for exhibition, generally speaking it is my practice to remove side buds about three weeks before a Show. If you like, it can be done gradually over a period of a month.

Where has all the scent gone? I'm not going to be drawn into a counting match and from this angle will merely say that there are quite enough of them to please any enthusiast. Rather am I going to be awkward and say quite definitely that scent is not all important. The most important factor is a strong and healthy grower and if it is scented so much the better. A poor untidy grower with no form in the flower given all the scent in the world plus the contents of a scent bottle can never be a good Rose.

My favourite Rose? How often is this question asked. Frankly I don't know, although I could possibly and more easily name a dozen. Each variety has its day and its year. Well do I remember cutting and winning with eighteen nigh perfect Mrs. Henry Bowles and, of course, to me on that day in London Mrs. Bowles was the finest variety in commerce. It never happened again but it has with other varieties. From the angle of perfect form of flower, Comtesse Vandal, McGredy's Yellow and Ivory and Golden Melody are to me still supreme. For pure garden effect, think of Violinista Costa and Cynthia Brooke. For the vase the free flowering and long stemmed President Hoover, Ena Harkness and Elite make them ideal, and a friend recently asked me for the *easiest* twelve varieties in colour more particularly for Box work. I should name Directeur Guèrin, The Doctor, Dr. Chandler, Emily, Golden Dawn, Golden Melody, McGredy's Ivory, McGredy's Pink, Peace, William Moore and the two new varieties, Gordon Eddie and Show Girl, most of which seldom produce a bloom of inferior form, and are capable of " holding " and travelling well. An additional red will be most useful and I would have no hesitation in suggesting Ena Harkness, for this variety is quite capable of being grown to " box " standard, and another variety that I have found most useful is the shrimp pink sport from Golden Dawn—East Anglia. It no doubt will be said that Golden Dawn throws quite a percentage of split blooms, a criticism that I do not contradict, but I still rank this variety very high, particularly for the number of blooms obtainable per tree, and as a consequence the wide choice available to find the good flower which has never caused me the slightest difficulty. I do not recall any case of staging a " twelve " without finding room for one of its kind. Of course there are others, but I'm sure these are among the easiest to grow ensuring a maximum selection of good blooms for the box.

Black Spot has caused a lot of trouble and argument for a year or two. We shall pass through the phase and meantime much can be done to prevent the disease. We are all such optimists, in June and July our trees are looking so good we can hardly bring ourselves to think of them being attacked, in fact in so many cases it's a matter of postponing the work of keeping clean until cleansing is necessary, for there is so much else to do. A most enthusiastic friend of mine who has not long been taking Rose growing seriously, but who now easily recognises the disease, suggested that possibly it had always been in her garden but that she had not taken any real notice of it. Maybe there is a lot of truth in this outlook, and after all the number of N.R.S. members studying these matters is enormous compared with twenty years ago.

A large number of the paler Roses, the creams and pinks, are persistently attacked by that quick moving insect, Thrips. I hardly feel such varieties are more susceptible than the warmer colours, but rather that the damage to the petal edge becomes more visible. If one takes the trouble to dust with D.D.T. in the green bud stage just as colour begins to show much damage will be prevented, the difficulty is remembering to do it. I find a small muslin flour bag most satisfactory for the purpose.

The Autumn work is falling upon us. With careful planning and attention to detail next July can bring all you desire in beauty of bloom so may I wish you good growing, good showing and no Black Spot, but do help on this wish with a preventative spraying because even a wish in the most sincere form will not make the spots grow less.

WILLIAM E. MOORE

President 1953

RED FAVOURITE. Floribunda (hyb. poly.)

Raised by M. Tantau, Germany. Distributed by Wheatcroft Bros., Ltd., Ruddington.

First Class Trial Ground Certificate 1952. Certificate of Merit Show Award 1951.

A ROSE GROWER'S PARADISE

THE VISCOUNT LYMINGTON, KENYA

WHEN I visited the offices of the National Rose Society, after my return from Kenya, I had no idea that I should be asked to write an article on Rose Growing in Kenya. In fact, if I remember rightly, most of our conversation was devoted to a discussion as to whether Floribunda was a proper nomenclature for certain types of Roses which are neither Hybrid Tea, nor strictly Hybrid Polyantha. Should this article ever reach the light of print, I hope those gardeners in Kenya, the majority of whom are far more qualified than I in my very short experience to write about it, will forgive me. I would like to say that this is mostly a collection of observations by an amateur over a very short time.

In Kenya it is far more difficult even than in England to lay down any hard and fast rule about Rose growing as the climate varies so much with height, and soils are very different all over the country. When I saw Mr. Bertram Park at Chelsea, I myself, rather unwisely, termed Kenya a rose-grower's paradise. There is no doubt that it is one, but probably by the time this article is finished it will seem to be more like a gardener's hell. However, is there a gardener in the entire world who has ever considered conditions absolutely perfect for him ?

I would first like to make some observations as to our climate. As I have said before, this varies very much with height ; our altitudes veer from sea level at Mombasa to 9,000 feet at Kinangop. All my experience has been at 6,000 feet with temperatures ranging from an average mean maximum of 74°F. by day to an average mean maximum of 52°F. by night. As you see, this lends itself to Rose-growing in hot-house conditions. Indeed, this " hot-house " simile applies to all but the highest areas of Kenya, where with frost at night the growing conditions more closely resemble those in England.

Soils. We have a good variety of soils ranging from 10-15 feet of rich volcanic top soil down to a foot or so of very poor sand. My own soil is a black loam which at first sight appeared to be mostly sand, but on further experience turned out to have a great deal of clay in it. One of the troubles in Kenya, with the torrential rains, is the wash, and in consequence any bed, which is remotely on a slope, has to be terraced. Heavy rains have also the effect, I believe, of washing the minerals and trace elements deep into the soil. Our richest soil, which lies on mountain slopes has, I believe, one fault. This soil is so rich that one tends to get too much sappy growth on bushes, which makes them extremely liable to bad attacks of Black Spot, our worst enemy. I suspect that all those living on this type of soil will disagree with me violently, but it does seem to me that whilst the mountain Roses are on the whole much better than the average " plains " Rose, their plants have a great deal more disease than ours.

Understock. The pH value of our soil is definitely on the acid side ; I would say roughly about 5.0 to 5.7. In consequence of this we have found Rosa multiflora or varieties of it the most suitable understock. Also, a good deal of the soil of Kenya is on the light sandy side. I think I am right in saying that with the exception of my friend, Grahame Bell, our oldest nurseryman in Kenya, and a man who has done as much for Kenya gardening as anybody, little work has been done in selecting the most suitable strains of understock. However, if someone could undertake this task I think it would be of the greatest value to the rose-growers of Kenya.

Planting. Planting in Kenya is normally done at the beginning of the rains ; the onset of which varies considerably all over the country. Our own rains in Kitale start usually at the end of March or the beginning of April. With adequate water one can plant at any time of the year, but those planted in the dry season never seem to do as well as those planted with the rains. When planting it is essential to bury the crown at least two inches below the surface of the soil as a protection from the direct rays of the sun. As a matter of fact, I have even seen bushes planted with the crown six inches below the soil and it seems to make little difference.

Growing. I would say that on the whole little use of artificial manures is made in Kenya. With the erosion we experience during the rains our most important job is the addition of humus in the form of compost, cattle manure, etc. I have, however, found it of great benefit to put a handful of bone meal into each hole when the bush is planted. Another most necessary piece of research I feel is the job of discovering a suitably balanced artificial manure to get the best out of our plants ; this, of course, to be used in conjunction with natural forms of manure. In our climate, Roses grow and bloom at what would seem to an English rose-grower a fantastic pace. There has been a great deal of discussion throughout the colony as to whether a period of dormancy is necessary to Roses, or not. As you can well imagine, dormancy in Kenya, if required, has to be induced as the seasons are not cold enough to produce it naturally, as in England. The normal way of inducing dormancy with us is to starve the plant of moisture during the dry season. However, in many cases this method seems not to have the slightest effect and Roses bloom the year round. There is a considerable body of opinion, with which I must say I am inclined to agree, which says that where there is no frost and therefore no need for Roses to protect themselves, it is unnecessary to make them go dormant. The argument against this is that without dormancy each year the life of the Rose bush is considerably curtailed. On the other hand, I have seen many gardens in which the owner assures me the Roses have gone on blooming the year round for ten years or more. I read with interest Mr. B. S. Bhatcharji's book on " Practical Rose Growing in India," where he considers it essential in the hotter parts of India that Roses should undergo a period of dormancy each year. I think it is possible that this would apply to our coastal regions, and his method of exposing a small part of the root system just under the ground is of great interest and might, I feel, be tried to advantage with us.

Pruning. With the exception of the cooler regions of Kenya, we employ long pruning. Pruning, however, is not all that easy when the plant makes ten feet or so of growth in one year, as did one of my President Hoovers, and one could scarcely get one's hand round the main stem.

Diseases. I should say that with the exception possibly of Red Spider, we suffer from all the usual Rose diseases. Black Spot is extremely virulent and once allowed to get the upper hand is almost unstoppable. However, with a lot of hard work and care it is possible to keep it in reasonable control, although it is very rare, if not impossible, to keep it out of the garden entirely. I have not yet tried the new oil emulsion sprays, but everyone over here seems to be enthusiastic about them and I have every intention of trying them next year. There is, I think, with our hot sun, a risk of burning the foliage. The methods I myself use for Black Spot are to spray once a week for three weeks before and four weeks after the beginning of the rains with Perenox ; after that every two weeks. There is also a small garden boy receiving a salary of 7/- per month whose sole job it is to take off every diseased leaf and twig and burn it. There is also no doubt that heavy mulching is extremely effective in controlling this disease. Mulching is also a wonderful deterrent to wash and erosion besides keeping the ground cool and, in the dry season, damp.

Mildew raises its ugly head usually towards the end of the dry season, that is, January-February with us. This seems a much more difficult disease to check. We have all tried lime sulphur, flowers of sulphur, bicarbonate of soda and the other 101 recommended chemicals, but there is always some mildew about during these months.

White ants are another serious pest and there is little one can do about it except to discover the nest, dig it up and destroy it, although used engine oil poured down their holes is said to be very effective. White ants appear mainly to attack young maiden plants ; once plants have established themselves and are growing well, white ants seem to prefer to leave them alone.

Our human pest is the garden boy. Of course, most people in England envy us in Kenya where we are able to have two or three gardeners at about 17/- a month each. However, the boys although on the whole good with vegetables, are not so keen on flowers and are unable to understand why on earth you should want to grow flowers as you cannot possibly eat them. If you are possessed of great patience and are prepared to sit down and show them the same thing a hundred times or so they do, on the whole, make fairly reasonable gardeners in the end. Just as you think that at long last you can trust the boy to do some particular job, he will go and make some completely childish mistake. There is a saying in Kenya that if there are 999 wrong ways of doing a job and one right, a boy will try each of the 999 wrong ways before he gets the right one. Perhaps some day we may have a school for training gardeners, who are always in great demand throughout the Colony where gardening is one of the bigger pursuits.

Showing. The standard of showing in Kenya is definitely a good deal below that in England, but it is, I believe, rapidly rising. I think there is no doubt that given the " know-how " our Rose Shows in Kenya would rival anything that England can produce. The trouble seems to be that we are not yet able to time, say, a box of six Roses so that each Rose can be shown in its best state. There is also a regrettable tendency to show in exhibition boxes, Roses which should not by any standard be called an exhibition Rose.

Varieties. Practically anything grows reasonably well and a great many better than they do in England. H.T., Teas, H.P. are all good. Hybrid Musks are excellent. Of the species Roses the Banksians and Rosa hugonis seem to be best. Most of the Ramblers do not grow at all well except in the higher parts ; Moss Roses are useless. Dwarf Polyanthas and Hybrid Polyanthas are both excellent. It is treading on dangerous ground to give a list of the best Roses in Kenya as they vary so much from district to district. For instance, Crimson Glory with us is all but useless, whereas round the shores of Lake Victoria I am told this variety usually takes the prize for the best Rose in the Show. However, here is a list of some of those that seem to do well :—

President Hoover, Peace, Daily Mail Scented (if anything the climbing form of this seems to be better than the bush), Climbing Mrs. Sam McGredy (the bush is almost useless), Angele Pernet, Mrs. George Geary, Etoile de Hollande, Climbing General MacArthur, Climbing Sunburst, Climbing Mrs. Aaron Ward, Joyous Cavalier, Mrs. Oakley Fisher, George Dickson, Julien Potin, McGredy's Ivory, Golden Dawn, Princess Marina, Comtesse Vandal.

The newer varieties have not yet had a fair trial with us, but so far Tahiti, Moonbeam, Charles Mallerin, Independence, Virgo, and Printemps, amongst others, look very promising.

Finally, I would like to say that rose-growing in Kenya is a delightful occupation as, to put it bluntly, one can almost put the Rose in upside down and three or four months later one has a remarkably fine bush. I have seen Roses treated in such a way that you would think it quite impossible for them to ever produce a bloom and a short time later you see the same bush again covered with more blooms than you would think it possible for any Rose to produce at one time. Perhaps one day we will have a Rose Society of our own, but until this happens we still rely on N.R.S. who are a very present help and the arrival of the Annual is an event eagerly looked forward to by most rose-growers.

EXHIBITING FOR BEGINNERS

A. NORMAN, Normandy

OF all the many kinds of flowers that are exhibited at shows, probably none is so exciting as the Rose.

Most flowers have a certain degree of latitude in their state of perfection. Some in fact, such as the Chrysanthemum, will remain in a perfect state for several days, which makes it much easier for the exhibitor who has perhaps only a limited number of plants from which to select his blooms. Furthermore, by manipulation of the plants, they can be induced to bloom at the required date, or at least thereabouts. In the case of Roses in the open garden very little can be done in this direction, as the weather will determine whether the blooms will be early or late. It is this fact that makes the exhibiting of Roses such an exciting business, for it must be realised that the Rose is in its highest phase of its possible beauty for just one day or so, and to show it in this state should be the aim of those who wish a First Prize card attached to their exhibit.

How is this desirable end to be achieved ? Here the choice of varieties is very important, whether the blooms are to be shown in the Decorative or Specimen Bloom classes in the Schedule.

Roses that have large and broad petals retain their form much longer than those with narrow and short ones. The number of petals is very little indication as to the lasting qualities of the bloom. For instance, Dame Edith Helen has a great number of petals—I have counted as many as eighty, and yet it must be cut young in order to keep it in its correct state. Varieties such as, for example, William Harvey, Red Ensign, McGredy's Ivory, Virgo, Sir Henry Segrave, Mrs. Charles Lamplough, Golden Melody, Rex Anderson, Show Girl, Dorothy Anderson, Leni Neuss, Elaine, Emily, Louise Crette, Candeur Lyonnaise and Mrs. Charles Rigg, all have large petals and retain the high pointed centre longer than many other varieties. The capacity to retain their form is governed to a great extent by the size of the blooms, for an increase in the size of the flower means that the petals are larger and wrap around one another and prevent the bloom from opening quickly. Although this is a great advantage it has also great drawbacks inasmuch as this type of Rose is very impatient of wet weather and will show its dislike by the petals sticking together and refusing to open. Fortunately this can be overcome by the use of the cone shaped shades made specially for the purpose. They are also useful for keeping off the effects of scorching sun.

With the possible exception of Virgo all the varieties I have mentioned are suitable for showing in the classes allotted to specimen blooms. For would-be exhibitors who have a preference for the Decorative classes, the following are some which would be found useful : President Hoover, Spek's Yellow, Lady Sylvia, Grand'mère Jenny, Verschuren's Pink, Lady Belper, Ena Harkness, Monique, Crimson Glory, Tallyho, Michèle Meilland, Opera, Rubaiyat and Sutter's Gold.

Cutting for the show

The time for cutting the blooms would be governed by the time at the disposal of the exhibitor and the distance of the Show place. Undoubtedly the best time for cutting is in the early morning of the day of the Show, for at this time the blooms, freshened by the dews, are at their brightest. Unfortunately, as our National Shows are held in London a journey of often considerable distance may be necessary, which means that, as one must reach the Show as early as possible in order to do justice to the exhibit, the blooms must be cut the evening before.

Blooms cut in the evening previous to the actual day of the Show must be less developed than those cut on the same day, unless it is about dawn, before the day's development begins. In June the daily development is somewhere between the hours of 6 a.m. and 9 a.m. and so it is obvious that a Rose which is cut in its full state of perfection before this development begins will be past its best in most cases on arrival at the Show.

Can the development of the blooms be arrested by tying their centres with thick wool or raffia as is sometimes done ? Personally I doubt it. I have tied blooms for very many years, but have at long last seen the futility of it. One of the great disadvantages associated with the tying of blooms is the false impression given on arrival at the Show, and it is not until the ties are removed that the value of the blooms can be appraised.

The important thing is to cut the blooms young enough so that the anxiety of knowing whether the blooms will stand or not will be removed.

The wiring of blooms is necessary in the case of some varieties which have rather weak foot stalks and also makes for easier arrangement in bowls or vases. Many of the decorative Roses do not require the use of wires, and it is possible that one day their use may be forbidden, except in the " artistic " classes.

After cutting, the blooms should be placed in deep receptacles so that their stems will be in at least six inches of water, and should be stood in the coolest spot that can be found for the night.

If it is proposed to show in the box classes, the blooms will be put straight into the boxes as soon as they are cut, as will also any spares in a special box for that purpose. Before putting the blooms in the boxes see that the tray is neatly mossed. Many beginners neglect this altogether, which is a pity for nothing enhances the look of the exhibit more than a well mossed box. In arranging the blooms place the largest one in the top left-hand corner and graduate them so that the smallest is in the bottom right hand. Alternate the colours as far as possible so that no two similar colours are together.

Transporting the blooms to the Show is one of the most important things in the whole business, for all the care given previously can be nullified by damage to the bloom in careless packing and transport. If one has a car to take the blooms to the Show, there should be little difficulty in getting them there in good condition, as the blooms need not be taken out of water. If, on the other hand, travelling by rail is the only means of transport, the blooms must be packed in boxes which can be easily carried. Those wooden florists' boxes are best suited for the purpose and will hold up to four dozen blooms if they have been disbudded. In order to ensure that the blooms will not move when the box is held on its side, pieces of stick or cane just a little wider than the width of the box can be wedged in position to hold the stems firm. Soft tissue paper should be used to line the boxes and every care should be taken to ensure that the blooms do not get wet by coming into contact with wet foliage. There are boxes made of cardboard which have the merit of lightness and ease of handling. To hold the blooms in position pieces of cane may be used and can be fixed across the stems with nails pushed through into the ends of the canes from the outsides of the boxes.

The Hybrid Polyanthas or Floribunda Roses are becoming very popular at the Shows. A certain amount of thinning of the buds about a week or so before the Show will prove to be advantageous. The object should be to have many buds on the trees of an even size so that the largest number of fresh blooms will be out at the same time, also to avoid showing trusses with stale stamens.

When showing in the vase classes some packing material is necessary in order that when the stems are placed in the required position they will stay put. Rushes are quite good, but have a habit of popping up as soon as the water is filled into the vase. Lonicera Nitida I find is by far the best, and is more readily available than rushes. Place the bundle in the vase, not too tightly, and cut off level with the top.

As a bloom is cut before its full development a certain amount of dressing will be necessary if the bloom is to be shown as it would be if left on the plant for a little longer. The colour of a Rose is nearly always more intense on the inside of the petals. This is particularly so in the case of the crimson varieties, so by bending the petals down, at the same time placing the thumb underneath, the petals will reflex. This operation will not only brighten the look of the bloom, but also enhance its size.

I would warn beginners, however, that to attempt to dress a bloom that is on the young side will give it an unnatural appearance, and it would be better to leave well alone. The removal of weather damaged guard petals is a practice usually frowned upon by the judges, although such a ruling does not appear in the Rules for Exhibitors. Sometimes it is only the edge of the petals which show defect, and in these cases they can be trimmed with a pair of scissors.

When showing in bowls, remember that the exhibit is to be viewed from all sides, so make a point of seeing that the blooms are disposed to this end.

Experienced exhibitors are always ready to help beginners, it being merely a matter of choosing the right time to ask for information. See that the Roses are correctly named, and the number of stems called for in the Schedule is not exceeded.

Success may not come at the first time of showing. If it does not, observe the reason, and try to do better next time. Remember, the most successful exhibitors were all beginners once, and it is only by constantly trying to improve the growing of the plants in their gardens, and mastering the art of exhibiting, that success has been theirs.

THE BICYCLE EXHIBITOR

E. E. GATWARD, Cambridge

THE above title may appear somewhat strange but it was suggested by my friends that an article on "Exhibiting for the Small Man" might be welcome. There have been a number of articles written in the past on this subject, but most of them appeared to have been written by Rolls-Royce exhibitors. You know them—those who travel to the shows in chauffeur driven cars with Roses nicely tucked away in a trailer at the back, but few seem to have been written by those who have "struggled," viz., the "Bicycle Exhibitor."

It is from this angle that I wish to write and the only excuse that I can offer for boring you is that I have been showing regularly in the smaller classes for some years now. I think my first exhibit was in London in 1929 and naturally over that fairly long period I have had a varied experience. Great pleasures tempered with a few disappointments, yet all eminently worth while.

To those who are hesitating on the brink wondering whether to take the plunge or not—I would say, "Do." I do not think you will regret it. After all, an exhibitor is an important person, for the Shows occupy a high position on the list of the Society's activities.

It goes without saying that first of all you must grow your Roses as well as ever you know how. You must in fact put a lot of time and a lot of thought into it for they will not just come. Yet if you love Roses and work for them they will come. Apart from the Shows you will get a great amount of pleasure in growing really lovely blooms, for that is what it means when you grow them well.

You must know the standard to be aimed at and in order to learn this may I suggest you make frequent visits, if you can, to the garden of a successful exhibitor, if one happens to live in your neighbourhood. Also you would learn a lot if you visited the Society's Shows before you commenced to exhibit yourself. This may not seem necessary to you but I can assure you that I have seen Roses brought to London from places situated a very long way off by exhibitors who obviously had not the faintest conception of the standard required or they would never have brought them.

When you do know the " standard " make it your own and do not fall below it. In other words do not exhibit Roses below your accepted standard in the hope that the competition is light and you will get away with it. It is not worth it and not worthy of you.

Mind you, many moons may wax and wane before you are able to grow and stage Roses like "B.P.," "R.W.," and "M.L.K.," all giants in the top classes to-day, but you *will* get them if you only keep on.

Before sending in your Entry Form, study the Schedule well before you finally decide on the Class or Classes you think would suit you best. As the decision has to be made a week before the Show and all kinds of weather may be expected before " The Day," this is not as easy as it sounds. To illustrate my point, a friend of mine told me only this year that he thought he might possibly be good in the Decorative Section but had little hopes for Specimen Blooms. A warm spell intervened and on the " Show Day " he was stronger in the Classes for Exhibition Roses than the Decoratives. You see what I mean.

I should imagine, that is if you are like me, you will find yourself walking round the beds " thousands " of times a day saying, " This will," " That might," and " That one never will be there." You will long to be able to arrange things so that the sun only shines on those fat buds that seem so long in coming and will miss those in another bed which do insist on galloping. That though is beside the point.

As you have, I hope, been working hard all the year it is most important that your effort is not lost through anything you do as the Show approaches. Be on your toes—watch your Roses—have everything ready. Boxes, wires, moss, etc., so that nothing is left to chance. Watch the weather also for it might pay you to cut on the morning before the Show rather than risk a storm. Remember that the Nurserymen have to. Unless compelled, owing to the fact that you live so far away, do not travel up to the Show overnight. If you can get there with say one and a half hours to spare and are not exhibiting in too many classes, your Roses will recover in water by that time and you will be all right. There *is* such a thing as being too tired before the Show and losing a certain amount of interest. That is fatal.

Much has been written about taking the Roses up in water. That is good if you have a car but not if you are a " Bicycle

Exhibitor." I have tried both ways, in water and in flat boxes, and I am convinced that if the Roses have been in water all the night before, they will travel equally well if they are carefully packed in a box so that they do not move about. Moss or wet paper round the bottom of the stems helps. I may say that only this year my wife travelled to London from Cambridge (52 miles) with a bunch of Roses in her arms and won the first prize in the Provincial Class at the Flower Show organised by the *Evening News*. So much for Roses in water.

Having arrived at the Show, first of all get the Roses in water again, that is essential. You can now breathe again and have a look round for your Class or Classes. Keep cool—pick up all the tips you can. This is now your most vital hour—remember that staging is a most important thing. Make the most of your Roses. Do not just put them up and leave them. Make the judges look at them and remember that first impressions count. A fellow exhibitor said to me only this year after we had been successful, " Your Roses were not *so* good, but your wife can stage Roses. You want to keep her." I did not tell him that I intended to. That reminds me, I have missed one of the best tips of all, and that is—if you are married do your very best by all the arts and crafts known to man to get her interested. Her help, advice and criticism will be invaluable and more than compensate you for that load of manure which you were hoping for but could not get.

I spoke earlier on about thrills and disappointments or something like that. Yes, you will get both.

I well remember winning my first card. It was a third and so thrilled was I that I sent a wire to my wife at home informing her of my success. That was a thrill.

I also remember, some years ago, staging Roses on a seaside pier. It was blowing, not a gale but a gale and a half. The vases were blown over and the blooms spoilt. To crown it all we staged in a marquee of green canvas. I have never seen such horrible Roses in all my life for they were greeny purple. That was a disappointment.

If these notes should persuade any of you to join us I shall be very happy—and if you do—please do not come into my Class. You might be too hot for me and I should be scared stiff.

THE CEREMONY OF THE ROSE AT HUNGERFORD

LEONARD HOLLIS, Morden

IN the Spring of 1952 some publicity was given to the ceremony of the presentation of a red Rose to Her Majesty on the occasion of her first visit to the town of Hungerford in Berkshire. The Constable of Hungerford, Major H. le F. Harvey, has kindly supplied an interesting historical background to the ceremony.

It seems that the tribute of a Rose to the Duke of Lancaster was not ordained by John o' Gaunt, who gave to the inhabitants of the town and manor rights of Common and valuable rights of Fishing. Disputes arose in the reigns of Henry VII and Elizabeth I as to the rights claimed by the inhabitants ; the Duchy attempted to abolish these rights and was stoutly resisted.

The original charter from John o' Gaunt disappeared in 1572, when the Constable of that time was involved in some underhand business, disposing of certain portions of the Manor. There was a long enquiry, which resulted in the prescriptive right of the inhabitants to fish on three days a week being upheld. The whole of the Manor passed to the inhabitants in 1613 when the Duchy was finally bought out, the Lordship of the Manor thereafter being vested in Feoffees for the benefit of the aforesaid inhabitants. This has continued to the present day, except that in 1908 Feoffees were replaced by Trustees when the Manor was vested in the Charity Commissioners.

The Constable's view is that the Red Rose is presented to the Reigning Monarch as a graceful tribute in commemoration of John o' Gaunt and possibly in remembrance of the fact that, after many years of dispute, the Manor passed from the Duchy to the inhabitants who had, generation after generation, maintained and asserted their rights.

The records and Constable's account books prior to 1820, as well as letters patent from Henry VI and Edward IV, are deposited at Reading with the County Archivist. Major Fairfax Harvey thinks that the presentation of the Red Rose is of comparatively recent origin, although now well established. The history of Hungerford does not mention it as appearing in the Constable's accounts, although various expenses were incurred when Queen Elizabeth I lay there (one of her coachmen had to be buried there). This, however, is not conclusive, as within living memory the Red Rose has been presented to Edward VII, George V, George VI and our present Queen, although the cost of the Rose has not appeared in the accounts ; past Constables, like the present one, were pleased to pay for the privilege.

Major Harvey also adds that there is a small piece of ground, granted in the 17th century as a playing ground for the children of the grammar school, for which a rent of a Red Rose was to be paid if demanded, and wonders whether this Rose was not the ancestor of the Rose now presented to the Reigning Monarch. It is an interesting speculation.

Incidentally it is worth recording that Charles I, Charles II, William of Orange, Queen Anne and George II all at various times stayed in or near Hungerford.

When Omar died the Rose did weep
Its petals on his tomb,
He would be laid where north winds keep
The Rose in freshest bloom.

When Sadi came, the child of song,
Each Rose flushed rosy red,
He sang their beauty all day long ;
With Roses crowned their head.

They shed no tear when Sadi died,
Aloft their scent they flung !
What matters Time or Death ? they cried,
Of us has Sadi sung !

Persian Poetry, translated by Anna Hills, 1884.

MOULIN ROUGE (hyb. poly.)
Raised by F. Meilland, France.
Distributed by Wheatcroft Bros., Ruddington, Notts.
First Class Trial Ground Certificate, Gold Medal and winner of the President's Cup, awarded for the best new rose of the year, 1952.
(For full description see page 150)

ROSES ON THE RIVIERA

JOSEPH BACCIALONE, HORTICULTURAL ENGINEER
Superintendent of the Gardens of Antibes, A.M., France
(*Translated by Bertram Park*)

AMONGST ornamental plants the Rose is certainly one of the most interesting on account of the great number of ways in which it can be used, of the multitude of its varieties, of its colour and of its refreshing perfume. The Rose is cultivated everywhere where the climate permits it to grow. In the garden or in the home, the Rose displays its grace in a way which no other flower can equal. The Mediterranean climate gives conditions and special possibilities for all kinds of horticulture. This applies to Roses as well as to all other kinds of cultivation.

In practice one is able to select for garden decoration special varieties of great richness for a dry climate. On the other hand our sunshine permits, with the simplest means, an important trade in the production of cut flowers which supplies the great French markets, Paris, Lyon, Bordeaux, Strasbourg, etc., and the foreign markets which are open to export in Germany, England, Sweden and Switzerland. Lastly in a special area, more industrial than horticultural, the Rose is cultivated for the production of flowers for perfume.

Before dealing with the subject, we must pay tribute to the memory of those to whom Mediterranean horticulture owes a large part of its richness by the hybridizations and introductions which they have accomplished ; Gilbert Nabonnand (1839-1903) and his sons and successors, Paul and Clement. We owe to them, for Roses in particular, a great number of varieties, which, after having made the fortunes of a great many cultivators of flowers, remain still, amidst other later introductions, some of the best Roses for warm and dry climates.

Antibes, at the present time, is the great centre for the production of Roses and Rose trees in the South of France. We meet there numerous cultivators who have almost industrialised their production as well as some true rosarians, Les Amis des Roses, Friends of the Rose, who assure the future of the culture of the Queen of Flowers.

The Production of Rose Plants in the South of France

Budding is the most usual method of propagation. The most suitable stock for our climate is Rosa indica major (R. odorata, Sweet) a climbing tree with deep coloured foliage, double pink flowers, sterile, and not perpetual. It is propagated by cuttings, which are taken after the 15th of August, of wood ripened by the August heat ; soft wood taken earlier gives plants lacking in vigour. One takes as cuttings the growths of the current year which have started from the base. They are usually about 28 to 40 inches long and of the thickness of a lead pencil. They are cut up into lengths of 12 inches, with an eye at the base, and they are defoliated. The stool plants are found in hedges bordering the fields, or the railroads, or are specially cultivated by the nurserymen.

Striking the Cuttings

The cuttings are placed in trenches in half shade, under the olive trees for instance, in furrows seven inches deep, and close together, 100 to the metre, are earthed up and watered copiously. In 20 to 40 days the cuttings have rooted. On lifting them from the trenches the eyes are cut out except the two at the top, and the roots are shortened. Then from October to March they are planted out in the nurseries. The planting out is made on ground that has been trenched, manured and levelled; it is divided into strips about 14 feet wide. The usual distance between the rows is about 14 inches and five to six inches between the plants. Other stocks used are R. canina which grows well here, but it suckers badly, and in cutting the suckers one cuts the roots, and the plant dies ; also its resistance to drought is limited. Multiflora de la Grifferaie, which is resistant to drought, is very vigorous, but its growth is capricious. The great advantage of R. indica major is that it reacts quickly to irrigation, so that one can regulate the growth of the plants at will ; no other stock possesses this characteristic.

Budding

Budding commences the first days of April with buds taken from plants grown under glass, for the varieties which are grown for the cut flower trade. The varieties for sale as garden plants are not budded until May, after the first great flowering. The budding is done about one and a half inches above the level of the soil with the usual technique. In about three weeks they have healed over and the " take " varies according to the variety from 50 to 95 per cent. On the average the number of usable plants does not exceed 70 per cent. of the cuttings planted. After budding the plants are irrigated copiously, and this is repeated twice weekly. Budding continues during the summer, with the scions growing well until the 15th of August, after which date, if they are still dormant, they are only rarely of interest. When the scion grows the raffia is cut and the stocks are cut back, the branches being trimmed down, but they are not headed back completely. The scions soon flower and then branch out, while the stocks which have not taken are budded again. A dressing of nitrate of soda or potash stimulates the growth. From the 15th of November the same year the plants are lifted for sale or for planting out. The Rose trees are taken to the shade, are defoliated, and the stocks are headed back to just above the cross cut of the T made when they were budded. The plants are packed in parcels of 5, 10 or 25 and sent away with careful packing to their destinations.

The greater number of the plants are destined for planting out for the cut flower trade, but certain specialists make collections of varieties for sale as garden plants. Out of a total of about 30 nurseries five or six are in this latter category. Sales are chiefly local but also to all the regions of the Mediterranean (France, North Africa, Egypt, etc.).

Diseases and Pests

These are few ; the Roses in the nurseries are liable to suffer from mildew, which is treated with one or two dustings of sulphur. The larvae of the cockchafer attacks the roots, but in general the strong growth prevents the larvae from doing serious damage.

Roses for Garden Decoration on the Côte d'Azur

In this climate under which we live, two important things have to be considered : (1) There are two periods of rest, the first in summer, in July and August, and the other in January-February ; (2) Our mild winters permit the employment of certain Roses both bush and climbing, which, susceptible to the cold of the north, grow admirably here and, moreover, have the great advantage of not suffering from the summer drought. One sees such varieties as the Tea Roses General Galliéni and Paul Nabonnand attaining five feet in height or Climbers of the Gigantea group with branches 30 feet long, and this without the plants receiving any special care or irrigation.

Truly in this region, in addition to its usual uses, the Rose constitutes a tree of choice to use in mass plantings, as hedges, as trimmed edgings, as isolated specimens, for arbours, etc., and they are in flower for ten months of the year. One sees unfortunately other trees more frequently (Spiraea and Oleander) which do not present the same qualities.

It should be noted that on the Riviera, the use of standard Rose trees is little utilised owing to the difficulty of finding a stock which gives a good stem. Canina has the faults already mentioned and R. indica does not root long cuttings. It would be necessary to make a double graft, as one does with fruit trees. It would need a good demand from their clientele for the nurserymen to find a practical solution.

The Culture and Care of Rose Trees in Pleasure Gardens

Planting is done between November and March in trenched and manured soil, at distances of 20 to 28 inches apart, and the graft level with the soil. Care is necessary to obtain good results ; mulching and manuring in spring, hoeing and watering in summer.

Pruning is a most important operation. One cuts out dead wood and prunes the good vigorous shoots to the third, fourth or fifth eye according to the strength and shape of the subject. From climbers one cuts out as much as possible of the wood which has carried flowers, and conserves the young growths, the date of the pruning determining the abundance of the flowering. The spring pruning takes place at the end of January, and there are no precise rules. Long pruning will give a large number of short flowering stems, which will transform the plant into a bush entirely covered with flowers, and will give a remarkable effect with the Tea Roses. In this case the flowering is precocious and commences in 70 to 80 days. On the other hand hard pruning will give fewer shoots, but these will be long and straight with fewer but larger flowers. This is the practice in growing for the cut flower trade, and is also applied to the varieties of Hybrid Teas and Pernetianas used in garden decoration. The flowering commences in this case after 100 days. In both cases numerous flowers open until the end of May, then there is a short period of rest, after which the Teas and Hybrid Teas recommence with a less abundant but continuous flowering, which sometimes lasts uninterruptedly all the summer, but is often stopped at the end of June by the heat. This is desirable and can be brought about if one wishes by discontinuing the watering.

About the 15th of August the branches are shortened and the trees evened up. Then watering is commenced again ; often indeed there is a period of rainy weather with less heat. Growth restarts again rapidly and at the end of September the flowering commences which will be prolonged in the case of the Teas until it is stopped by the frost in January. This autumn flowering is often more beautiful than that of May. Rest periods are short or non-existent, and a carefully planned pruning programme will give Roses in continuous flower throughout the year.

The Most Interesting Varieties for Gardens

The number of varieties is immense and new ones are continually being introduced. It is necessary to say frankly that these novelties can only be accepted with caution in our region and only after special trials, because the climate puts them in difficulties during three or four months of the year ; artificial watering only imperfectly replaces the natural rainfall. To succeed one must rely on those varieties which have proved their merit. These varieties although they may be already old, have not become outmoded, but at the same time one must not exclude the novelties, some of which are remarkable and possess all the required qualities.

Of the bush Roses we give first of all a high and very important place to the Tea Roses, those old Roses which are so precious here, with their continuous flowering and beautiful, persistent, sometimes reddish foliage. Their flowers have not the size and refined elegance of modern Roses ; they are of medium size only but very double, highly perfumed and most graceful both in their delightful buds as well as in their open flowers. Their profusion is such that in April-May and again in October the plants almost disappear under the flowers and thanks to a continuous remontancy, whether the season be dry or cold there are always flowers to be found.

Among the very numerous varieties, we will mention Archiduc Joseph, carmine rose ; General Galliéni, flame red ; General Schablikine, copper red ; Mme. Antoine Mari, pink ; Souvenir de Gilbert Nabonnand, coppery chamois.

The Bengal Roses such as Alice Hamilton and Sunny South are interesting for landscape effects and for hedges.

The Hybrid Perpetuals are very resistant to climatic changes and give a good flowering twice a year ; Gloire Lyonnaise, Ulrich Brunner and General Jacqueminot are grown.

The Hybrid Teas are successful nearly everywhere and are continuous in their flowering. Among them may be noted : Grüss an

Coburg, Dame Edith Helen, Prince de Piémont, Gloire d'Antibes, Rouge Meilland (Happiness) and Eclipse.

The Pernetianas are much affected by the heat and sometimes have a short life. Among the more interesting are Condesa de Sástago, Padre, Talisman, Opera, and Saigon.

The Hybrid Polyanthas (Floribundas) succeed well, particularly Orange Triumph.

Of the climbing Roses, those most used on the Riviera are the very vigorous types which are able to cover large spaces of wall or trellis.

Amongst the Wichuraianas, one may mention Paul's Scarlet, and among the Species there are seen R. anemoneflora, and the Banksian Roses both White and Yellow.

In the Gigantea class is La Folette, and among the Climbing Tea Roses, Noella Nabonnand. Bourbons : Mme. Ernest Calvat. Noisettes : Reve d'Or. Climbing Hybrid Teas : Iréne Bonnet, Lady Waterlow and Marie Nabonnand which is one of the most beautiful climbing Roses of the Midi. Climbing Bengals : Cramoisi Superieur and Gloire de Rosomanes. In general the climbing sports of the Hybrid Teas (Mme. Abel Chatenay, etc.) have little vigour and are only interesting as part of a collection.

BOOK NOTES

“ **Anyone Can Grow Roses.”** By Cynthia Westcott. 150 pages, illustrated. (Macmillan and Co., Ltd.), 15/-. Dr. Cynthia Westcott has studied and written about plants, and particularly plant pests and diseases, for many years, and has become one of America's best known plant pathologists. Known as the plant doctor, her greatest enthusiasm has always been the Rose, and this book condenses years of study and practice, and the result of long experience in her own test gardens, with all the new varieties and pest controls. Written in simple language, this is a book for every Rose gardener, and while some of it applies only to conditions prevailing in the United States of America, the general principles are universal.

“ **The Rose : A quarterly journal for all Rose Lovers.”** Price 2/-. This new magazine of convenient pocket size and devoted exclusively to Roses and Rose gardening made its first appearance with the October, 1952, issue. Well illustrated with four-colour plates and many in monochrome, its 74 pages are well filled with useful information which is of helpful interest to all who grow Roses. We give it our very best wishes and look forward to future issues.

THE ROSE GARDENS AT BAGATELLE

E. M. COCKBURN, KEW

NO Rose lover visiting Paris should fail to visit the delightful Rose garden at Bagatelle in the Bois de Boulogne. The adjoining photograph was taken towards the end of May when the gardens were being prepared for the annual competition for new Roses which is held in June.

Bagatelle combines the charm of an established Rose garden with all the interest and excitement which surround a trial ground for new Roses. The small beds which contain the new Roses are about a yard long and each bed bears a small notice giving the raiser's name. At a time when so many of the best new Roses are of French origin—Peace, Michèle Meilland, Mme. Yves Latieule (adjudged Medal Bloom at the 1952 N.R.S. Summer Show) and many more come to mind—it is interesting to go to Bagatelle to see how the French display their Roses. On my visit in May many of the climbing Roses grown against a wall were in full bloom, and I was impressed by the charming contrast offered to them by the clematis with which they were interspersed.

The 1952 competition at Bagatelle proved to be a triumph for Monsieur and Madame Mallerin. Not only did they win the Gold Medal with Flambée (a floribunda of a brilliant flame colour) but also the second prize with Baiser (an H.T. Type whose colour is described as " rose porcelaine satinée ") and the Decorative Rose Certificate with Tonerre, a floribunda of garnet red with violet reflections. If the recent successes of Frensham, Fashion, Vogue, Masquerade and many others are any criterion, it would seem that the Floribunda Roses which have many of the attractions of the shrub for the Rose lover who is his own gardener, will soon be challenging the supremacy of the Hybrid Tea Type in our Rose gardens.

To finish on a practical note, La Roseraie de Bagatelle is on the west side of the Bois de Boulogne—to the car driver it presents no difficulties, but it is not easily accessible by Metro. The nearest stop is Pont de Neuilly, from where a taxi will take you to the gardens in five minutes.

THE BAGATELLE GARDENS, BOIS DE BOULOGNE, PARIS

Concours International de Roses Nouvelles de Bagatelle, 1952
List of Awards

Bagatelle Gold Medal. " Flambée," raised by Charles Mallerin. Floribunda, deep red with " fiery " reverse.

Premier Certificat. " Baiser," raised by Mme. Mallerin. Hybrid Tea Type, bright pink, marbled with brick red.

Bagatelle Certificate. " Naples " (nom provisoire), raised by F. Meilland. Hybrid Tea Type, ochre yellow tinted turkey red.

Bagatelle Certificate. " Buccaneer," raised by H. C. Swim, Armstrong Nurseries, California. Hybrid Tea Type, light yellow.

Certificate for Decorative Rose. " Tonerre," raised by Charles Mallerin. Floribunda, garnet red, deep but brilliant, a new colour in Roses.

THE ROSE IN DESIGN

BETTY K. BATTERSBY

Very old are the woods;
And the buds that break
Out of the briar's boughs,
When March winds wake,
So old with their beauty are—
Oh, no man knows
Through what wild centuries
Roves back the Rose.

WALTER DE LA MARE.

TRULY the Rose is of most ancient origin. There have been found in Central Oregon and Colorado fossil deposits suggestive of Rose leaves, fruit, bud and a portion of stem with thorns, estimated to be at least 35 million years old, and in the Rose Museum at L'Häy les Roses near Paris are some fossils of identifiable Rose species in chalk of the cretaceous age.

Paleolithic men, who were responsible for those wonderfully skilful drawings of animals still to be seen in the caves of Altamira, seem rarely to have depicted plant life. An unusual example is the delicate drawing of leaves scratched on bone illustrated in Mr. Wilfrid Blunt's book "The Art of Botanical Illustration," but there is no reason why we, like the poet, should not imagine the Rose, protected by thorns, blossoming through the long forgotten centuries.

Indian Rose

In recorded history, we have proof that the Rose was used in Babylonian and Assyrian architecture and decoration. Sargon, King of Babylonia *c.* 2845-2768 B.C., sent to Akkad, the capital of his empire "two species of fig trees, vines, Rose trees and other plants." The earliest known European representation of the Rose dates from 1700 B.C. and is in the House of Frescoes at Knossus, Crete.* In this illustration the

* See illustration in colour in "The Rose Annual" of 1937.

Persian Rose

flowers and leaves are conventionalised, the flowers having six petals, and being of a golden rose colour with orange centres dotted with deep red. Another example is that in the four main courts forming part of the palace of Nebuchadnezzar II (about 600 B.C.), where were columns "supporting a broad band studded with white Roses on an azure ground and blue lozenges outlined in yellow."

"Rosette" motifs are found in the ornament of Egypt, Assyria, Greece and Pompeii, but whether a flower, a wheel or even a star was the original inspiration of these "rosettes" we can only guess. There seems no limit to the "petals" of these early "rosettes." Egyptian flower heads are commonly four or eight petalled, Assyrian eight, ten or twelve, Greek seven, eight, nine or fifteen.

Herodotus, the Father of History, *c.* 480 B.C., gives the first account of a double Rose in the gardens of Midas, "in which wild Roses grew, each one having 60 leaves, surpassing all others in fragrance." It is generally thought that this was the Rosa centifolia.

Theophrastus (*c.* 372-280 B.C.), the pupil of Plato and Aristotle, in his "Enquiry into Plants," discusses the Rose : "Among Roses there are many differences, in the number of petals, in roughness, in beauty of colour, and in sweetness of scent. Most have five petals, but some have twelve or twenty, and some a great many more than these : for there are some, they say, which are even called 'hundred-petalled'."

Poets and writers throughout the centuries have praised the Rose. Pliny in his Natural History mentions 12 varieties of Roses, and classical scholars quote countless references from the works of Virgil, Horace, Juvenal, Cicero and others. Lovers of lyrical poetry will remember references by Marlowe, Shakespeare and Herrick.

In Roman times the Rose was regarded as an emblem of love and

Heraldic Rose

interesting tracery and brilliant colour of " Rose " windows, many of which date from the 13th century.

The Rose motif was much used in tapestries of the late 15th and early 16th centuries. Brussels and Franco-Burgundian works had borders of a stylised Rose with foliage, and those of Tournai show dog Rose bushes clearly depicted in the general composition.

Examples of work of this period examined at the Victoria and Albert Museum include a German cope, where charming motifs of flowers, buds and leaves are delicately worked in gold, silver and coloured silks, and an English cushion cover embroidered in wool and silk on linen depicting stylised Persian Rose trees together with the Tudor Rose ; but there are, of course, countless historical examples of the flower, and designers will wish to study museum specimens suitable for their own particular craft.

The 17th century saw the Rose develop as a popular motif in practically every craft. One of the more unusual was in leather wall hangings of Italian or Spanish origin, where the motif was embossed and then painted naturalistically. Wooden panelling was also frequently decorated with both stylised and free painted or carved Roses. An arm-chair of this period in the Victoria and Albert Museum is covered with " Turkey Work " in a design of stylised Rose trees. It is interesting to note how the craft of embroidery, famous in this country since Norman times, displays in great variety the many decorative aspects of the Rose.

Furniture of the 18th century was heavily ornamented, and the Rose played an important part in this decoration. Table tops were worked in scagliola depicting natural Roses ; chests and bureaux bore bouquets of painted Roses, and the flower was frequently used in carvings.

Textiles of this period show both printed and woven designs, and Roses were again a frequently used and important motif. Chintzes and wallpapers inspired by Chinese designs carried delicate oriental versions of the flower, and it also appeared in French " Toile de Jouy."

Artists and designers of to-day will add to the praise and beauty of the Rose by studying it afresh. By their skill and artistry they will bring the flower to life again, so that, in the words of Gerard the Herbalist, " the Rose doth deserve the chiefest and most principall place among all flowers."

THE LATE TRANSPLANTING OF ROSES

R. L. PALLETT, SURREY

I SUPPOSE that most Rosarians agree that the best time for the transplanting of Roses of all types is at the beginning or at the end of their normal dormant period, that is to say either from late October to mid-December or from late February to the end of March.

Quite often, in warm and early springs, growth has advanced by mid-April to such an extent that Roses are very far from dormant and although it is true that with great care they may be transplanted even in full summer growth, and survive, the shock is usually so great that they never again fully recover their old vigour.

It is, however, late spring transplanting with which I have been recently concerned, and the results may be of interest to those who find themselves in the position, as I did this spring, of having to move house, and contents of garden, well after the ideal time.

I was to take over the new property in mid-May, but this was considered dangerously late should hot dry weather set in at that time and in fact that did happen, temperatures well in the 70s being experienced in the shade with hot sunshine for nearly two weeks.

Permission was therefore sought and obtained to move the Roses to the new garden in the last week in April.

The trees to be moved included established bushes and standards, bushes and standards budded the previous year, and several established bushes of the species. Most of the bushes were on briar, a few on laxa. The standards were on briar and rugosa.

A few days before the lifting date a clean sharp spade was pushed vertically into the soil some six inches from the base of each plant, to cut spreading roots and the spade rocked backward and forward a little to loosen the soil somewhat. This was done with a view to reducing the subsequent shock when the plants were lifted.

When the lifting day came, a quantity of well soaked fine peat was ready with pieces of old sacking, also thoroughly wet. The day was very warm and sunny and an early start was therefore made.

First the bushes budded the previous year, some of which were well started into growth, were lifted and packed tightly in boxes, a layer of Roses and a layer of wet peat alternating. Similarly the bush Roses were lifted and packed in the wooden boxes, all as tightly as possible. As they were filled the boxes were placed in the shade and covered with wet sacks.

The standards were carefully lifted, one at a time, and with the least possible delay packed into a heap of peat placed in the middle of a piece of wet sacking until manageable bundles were assembled when the sacking was then tied up as high as possible round the stems and the bundles stood in the shade. Particular care was taken with the standards budded the previous year since in many cases growths were already several inches long, and although tied in to canes could very easily have been damaged.

The bush species were packed in boxes with peat in a similar way to the ordinary bushes.

With the exception of the species all the wood on all trees was left uncut in any way, although moderate pruning had been carried out on the established trees some weeks previously at normal pruning time. The species had to be cut well back to make them manageable.

The whole collection was repeatedly sprayed with water throughout the day of lifting and early on the following day when they were to be moved to their new quarters.

The hot weather had, by the evening of the lifting day, caused the larger growths on the maiden standards to become very limp despite the regular watering and overhead spraying, but it was with great satisfaction that I found them quite firmed up again the following morning.

The local florists' van had been chartered and as early as possible on the second day the Roses were taken to their new garden. Here no previous preparation had been possible and shallow trenches were therefore opened in the vegetable garden and the older trees heeled in, a few inches apart and well firmed. The standards were placed in a separate trench and the heads fastened to a wire stretched between two posts. The dwarf maidens were carefully planted out in rows, a foot apart, and six inches apart in the rows and the whole collection were then left to fend for themselves until the move into the house took place in mid-May. The reason for the close planting for the first year was that it was thought that growth would be somewhat stunted the first year in any case and the shade from the foliage would be of greater benefit than if the usual spacings had been allowed. The present station is a temporary one and with the trees close together in one part of the garden subsequent watering has been easier. In the autumn the collection will be planted out in prepared beds.

As I write, in mid-June after a period of eight weeks which included two hot dry weeks in May, the trees are, generally, looking very satisfactory.

Rather unexpectedly, the least evidence of the late move is shown by the maiden rugosa standards, many of which have thrown long and strong shoots while none has failed. The maiden bushes, on briar, have also taken well, 95 per cent. are growing, although naturally not with the vigour of undisturbed maidens, but a few have already bloomed. The established standards, on briar, have suffered most—they were budded in 1947/8/9—the old growth has died back in some cases rather badly, but on the stems near the stock buds are already breaking and a fair recovery is expected. Success with the established dwarfs has varied, but as might be expected is related to the length of time that they have been settled in the old garden. All are alive and growing but bushes planted last year are responding much more quickly than their settled-in neighbours.

Much advice was sought from fellow Rosarians before the move took place and the advice and opinion varied greatly. Many forecast that the "just starting" maidens would suffer badly, in fact they suffered least. Some said that standards would be difficult, in fact rugosa standards moved well, briars not so well. Some said cut hard back before, some after the move, others advised leaving all growth untouched. In fact all growth was left intact, the argument being that the sap in the old wood would tend to resist the drying out of the buds at the base of the plant.

To sum up—when moving late in the season and particularly when summer weather has already arrived, the greatest possible care must be taken to see that at all times there is no possibility of drying out and exposure of the roots to the air should be cut down to the absolute minimum. The value of wet peat cannot be over-emphasised as a packing material and for adding to the soil with and about the plants when planting.

Finally, and possibly most important of all, firm planting is advocated at all times ; in late planting it is an essential.

FIRST LOVE (H.T.)
Raised by Herbert C. Swim, Armstrong Nurseries, California, U.S.A.
Distributed by R. Harkness & Co., Hitchin, Herts.
First Class Trial Ground Certificate and Certificate of Merit, 1952.
(For full description see page 149)

ROSE VARIETIES

EDWIN de T. BECHTEL, NEW YORK

AMONG horticulturists, the term " variety " is applied to cultivated plants—hybrids and bud mutations. A variety is a group of plants related by descent, but distinguished from other similar groups by characteristics too inconstant or too trivial to entitle the group to recognition as a species. This language is as old as Darwin and Asa Gray. The definition of a species, on the other hand, is much more difficult. It is a category of botanical classification, the determination of which formerly depended on a study of external traits and the form and structure of preserved specimens. To-day such comparative morphology is supplemented above all by observations of cell structure under high-powered microscopes which reveal the intricacies of the nuclei, chromosomes and genes of cells ; but, nevertheless, the definition of the term " species " continues to be very troublesome, especially in the classification of Roses. At most, botanists tend to adopt working empirical classifications and denominate, as species, groups of plants which possess, in common, one or more characteristics distinguished from other similar groups, with the ability to interbreed and to reproduce their characteristics in their offspring.

The June number of the Magazine of the American Rose Society has just arrived ; it announces the two Roses which have won the All-American Rose Awards for 1953. The winners are Chrysler Imperial, a crimson red hybrid tea, and Ma Perkins, a sparkling coral-shell pink Floribunda or Hybrid Polyantha. The blooms of Chrysler Imperial are said to be beautifully formed, having about fifty petals, and will keep remarkably well. It was originated by Dr. Walter E. Lammerts, an accomplished and distinguished hybridist. The rose had as its parents, Mirandy and Charlotte Armstrong, which were All-America winners in earlier years. E. S. Boerner, who is also an accomplished and distinguished Rose hybridist, originated the Floribunda, Ma Perkins, by crossing Red Radiance and Fashion. Red Radiance is one of the famous and almost foolproof Hybrid Teas, and Fashion is a Floribunda or Hybrid Polyantha which made its bow so brilliantly two years ago when it took the highest honours at the Bagatelle International Competition at Paris.

These Roses were given tests in twenty All-America Rose Award trial gardens for two years. Preceding these tests, seven or eight years of planning and actual labour was involved in bringing these Roses into being after hybridization and in determining their final selection after planting, observing, sorting and discarding thousands of seedlings.

On the subject of discarding seedlings and the probable success of hybridizing, figures prove that the chance of securing a good new variety has been as encouragingly low as 1 to 160, and as hopeless as 1 in over 1,000. For example, there is an instance of the ripening of some 6,000 crosses into 80,000 seeds, from which some 40,000 seedlings were grown. These, in turn, were checked, and so many were discarded that only 1,600 plants were left. Out of this residuum, six Roses were finally selected and qualified as successful new variations.

And now to continue the genealogy of our two All-America Winners : Mirandy, one of the parents of Chrysler Imperial, is the daughter of a famous McGredy Rose and of Charlotte Armstrong (also one of the parents of the new Rose). Charlotte Armstrong is the daughter of Soeur Thérèse and of Crimson Glory.

All of these Roses are tetraploids (having 4×7 chromosomes) as compared with the usual cell structure of Roses ; for they are generally diploid (having 2×7 chromosomes in every cell). Rose cells—and there are millions in a single Rose—are made up of nuclei, chromosomes and genes which are supposed to carry the hereditary characteristics. As the cells of Roses mature to a maximum, they divide into two parts, each containing one half of the chromosomes and genes ; and each new cell as it develops receives one of the equal parts. In plant reproduction, one half of the diploid chromosomes, or 7, or one half of the tetraploid chromosomes, or 14, goes to the feminine seed-producing pistil of the Rose and one half to the masculine pollen members ; for the Rose is an hermaphrodite. When the pollen of one Rose variety is transferred in hybridization to the pistil of another Rose, there is a union of the chromosomes by the combining of the pollen (stamen) and seed-producing (pistil) cells, if the crossing is fertile. This union restores chromosomes to the original diploid or tetraploid number. Roses in general do their fractions and accounting very well indeed. It is sometimes found, however, that the use of the alkaloid *colchicene* stimulates the fertility of chromosomes and increases their number. The use of other drugs as well as radiation also stimulates the chromosomes. Plants having such chromosomes are apt to behave in unusual ways. Artificial aids to hybridization thus give promise of a new technique of Rose breeding and culture.

And now—to return to our new Rose, Chrysler Imperial. The grandparent, Soeur Thérèse, is the daughter of Souvenir de Claudius Pernet, one of the yellow Pernetiana Roses derived out of the famous Soleil d'Or, which was the first Pernetiana Rose originated by Pernet-Ducher in 1900. That origination is responsible for the variegated colors of our modern Hybrid Teas, even including our Rose Peace, or Mme. A. Meilland, as Peace is called in France.

The other grandparent of Soeur Thérèse, however, is an unknown seedling. Crimson Glory, another grandparent of our new Rose, Chrysler Imperial, is a descendant through a complicated line, and by way of the famous Hybrid Tea, Liberty, goes back to the great Roses, Mme. Victor Verdier, Général Jacqueminot and Lady Mary Fitzwilliam. But the line is frequently broken by the crossing of an unknown seedling.

Genealogically the other All-America winner, Ma Perkins, the daughter of Fashion and Red Radiance, has Pinocchio and Crimson Glory as antecedents on the one hand, and Radiance, Mme. Caroline Testout, Lady Mary Fitzwilliam and Liberty on the other. But the lines of our pedigrees are broken again and again by the crossing of the inevitable unknown or unnamed seedlings.

And then, in turn, back of all these ancestors are the many varieties which developed and flourished throughout the 19th century : (1) the earliest Gallica hybrids ; (2) the Bengal or China hybrids ; (3) the Bourbon hybrids ; (4) the Portland or Perpetual Damask types ; (5) the Tea Roses ; (6) the Hybrid Perpetuals.

All these Roses I have mentioned are varieties.

And now let us examine a few Rose generations directly out of species Roses. A beautiful American species is the *Rosa setigera*, with its curving lyre-shaped branches and its delicate pink to cream-color blooms, which cover the bushes with clusters in late July and August. This is one of the 25 American species. *Rosa setigera* was crossed with *Rosa foetida bicolor*, and produced Doubloons, a climber with very large double-cupped, fragrant, rich golden clusters of flowers. Another hybridization of *Rosa setigera* was successful over 100 years ago, when Feast originated Baltimore Belle, a famous old rose, very double, fragrant, pale blush with clustered blooms. Another origination by Feast was Queen of the Prairies. Both resulted from the crossing of *Rosa setigera* with *Rosa Gallica,* a most flirtatious and lovely species Rose and very prolific in hybrid form.

Interesting experiments have been made at Canadian agricultural experiment stations in an attempt to cross *Rosa setigera* with some of the indigenous, rugged and winter-hardy Canadian Rose species, with the hope of producing a Rose to withstand the frigid weather of north-western Canada. For this purpose, another species Rose, *Rosa rugosa rubra* (*R. rugosa typica*), has been tried out without very much success in producing a type of super-hardy Rose. On the other hand, American hybridists have been extraordinarily successful in originating many types of beautiful Rugosa hybrids which are very vigorous in our latitude. They include such favourites as Agnes, Stella Polaris, the silvery pink Conrad Ferdinand Meyer, its tall white sport Nova Zembla, and Dr. Van Fleet's hybrids, including his rose pink Sarah Van Fleet. Indeed Dr. Van Fleet was responsible for more than 25 successful originations out of the *Rosa rugosa* species, *Rosa wichuraiana,* etc. Among the American hybridists who have used these species with great success are Horvath, the Brownells, Bowditch, and others.

And thus we might attempt to follow interesting crossings and intricate genealogical ascents and descents almost indefinitely ; for hybridization, which began as a natural crossing of species, has been carried on intricately and often hectically since Dupont made his first experiments in Empress Josephine's garden. Of course, the Rose species are a widely distributed genus, extending through the northern hemisphere as far south as Mexico on our continent, in Africa as far south as Abyssinia, and in Asia to southern India. The age and distribution, the habit and characteristics of this genus are responsible for the fact, acknowledged again and again by the botanists, that there is no botanical genus, the number and characteristics of whose species are so difficult to determine.

Linnaeus described 14 species in 1762, but soon changed to 21. The English, French and Dutch botanists made various guesses.

In 1820, an extraordinary genius at 21 published his system of Rose classification. This is John Lindley's *Rosarum Monographia*, one of the great books of botany. It comprises 11 sections with 76 sub-divisions as species and sub-species. This classification prepared the way for that of M. Crépin at the end of the last century. He was the director of the Brussels Botanical Garden, and divided the Rose genus into 15 sections and 55 species. Prof. Bailey in his *Cyclopedia of Horticulture* approved the modification of Crépin's system. It has 15 sections and 60 major sub-divisions. Dr. McFarland in his *Modern Roses III*, 1949, adopts Prof. Rehder's classification, which includes 266 species. In the Royal Horticultural Society's new *Dictionary of Gardening*, which has just been issued, the total number of species is given at about 125, of which 95 are Asiatic, 18 are American, and the remainder are chiefly natives of Europe or north-western Africa.

And what becomes of the Roses of our gardens, the cultivated Roses, in the wake of these complicated theories of classification ? We have mentioned Hybrid Teas, Hybrid Polyanthas, Hybrid Rugosas. Of course, none of these forms are found or referred to in the botanies ; they have no scientific status ; for the botanist is not interested in hybridized, cultivated Roses. We have noted how mixed and uncertain is their genealogy and how broken are their pedigrees. Thory, the author of Redouté's text, calls the hectically produced Gallica hybrids of his time, "*monstres*." They were *métis*, mongrel, half-caste, half-bred, the product of "*hybridité adultérine*." But, in spite of these irregular flirtations and in spite of the paternity of unnamed and unknown seedlings and the breaking of the laws of the scientists, hybridizations and the origination of new types have been responsible for the popularity of the Rose and the fascination and beauty of its hybrids. Miscegenation has been pursued freely and gaily, and new forms, new varieties of Roses have increased multitudinously from year to year since Empress Josephine became the patrone of Roses at Malmaison.

In 1902, when M. Gravereaux listed the Roses which he planted in his famous Roseraie de L'Häy, near Paris, his total was 6,759 species and varieties. There were 1,690 Hybrid Perpetuals and only 271 Hybrid Teas. In 1906, Simon and Cochet gathered from all sources available to them, past and present, all known Rose names.

The total of their extensive list was 11,016, or over 9,000 varieties, after allowing for duplications.

The infinite varieties are, of course, due to the structure of the Rose cell and the intensity of Rose hybridizing and Rose culture since the days of Malmaison. First in Empress Josephine's time came the unrestrained encouragement of the seedlings of the natural crosses of the Gallicas. Varieties, bizarre, striped, spotted and mottled, as well as the beautiful Agatha Gallicas which are illustrated by Redouté, came and disappeared, although some of the finest Gallica hybrids persisted until the first decade of this century. Following the Gallica hybrids came the Bengal or China hybrids resulting from the crossing of *Rosa chinensis semperflorens* with Damasks, Centifolias and the Gallicas themselves. The Bengal or China hybrids became popular and were planted in many gardens in the United States in great numbers in the first half of the last century. The Bourbons were another French origination. They resulted from the natural pollination of the common China Rose with the monthly Damask. That hybrid was also very popular in the United States during the last century ; and the Souvenir de la Malmaison, the Hermosa and the Gloire des Rosomanes still represent the Bourbons.

In the meantime, there was much experimentation to stimulate the Damask strain. The resulting Damask Perpetuals were very successful, and the Rose du Roi was advertised by Buist of Philadelphia as guaranteed to bloom " profusely and perfectly from June until Christmas."

Out of these varied hybrids came the strains of the Hybrid Perpetuals. Vibert and Laffay hybridized Gallicas, Bengals, Bourbons, Damasks, and, turning back to *Rosa chinensis semperflorens* and the Damask Perpetuals, managed to originate the vigorous and beautiful remontants, the Hybrid Perpetuals. Probably Laffay's Princess Hélène, a cardinal red Rose which dated from 1837, is the first Hybrid Perpetual. His originations, which continued up to the middle of the last century, were prolific ; and he and Vibert established the status of the Hybrid Perpetual. At first it was regarded as something of a parvenu because many of its new originations would not repeat dependably. However, by 1860, it was established and became the world's favorite Rose variety for over half a century. Even as late as 1902, Gravereaux could find 1,690

Hybrid Perpetuals for his garden at L'Häy as against 296 Teas. Among these Hybrid Perpetuals, I pay special tribute to Georg Arends, Henry Nevard, Ulrich Brunner, Baroness Rothschild, Louise Cretté, Général Jacqueminot and Paul Neyron ; and to add a sister who was not originated until the 19th century, one of the best white Roses, Frau Karl Druschki. And these are only a few of the beautiful collection of 104 Hybrid Perpetuals in the New York Botanical Garden, which I checked and described three years ago.

As to the next class of varieties, the Hybrid Teas, their first origination came in 1867 when La France made its bow. The unusual Cheshunt Hybrid, originated by G. Paul in 1872, was the first Hybrid Tea generally recognised as such. Actually, the career of the Hybrid Teas in Europe was slow in its consummation, as was the case of the Hybrid Perpetuals. Even at the beginning of this century, the Hybrid Tea was looked upon as a tender variety unable to live in the rigorous climate of the United States. Its popularity and the general success of Hybrid Teas owes much to the use of *Rosa multiflora* as an understock. But the discussion of understocks still continues ; for we need more sturdy Hybrid Teas.

To-day our most recent and most popular classes of varieties are the Hybrid Polyanthas or Floribundas. But it is a long and complicated story which deserves a separate paper. Of course, the name Hybrid Polyantha or Floribunda does not accurately describe this astonishing and beautiful category of new varieties. There is great need of revising and defining Rose varieties in general.

Of the Rose and the multiplicity of her forms, we can appropriately say :—

> " Age cannot wither nor custom stale
> Her infinite variety."

Alas ! Many of the great varieties are falling out of the ranks of the army of Roses and are disappearing. We should try to preserve the best representatives of all varieties. They need friends and sanctuaries in public parks and in your own gardens. They should be cherished for their beauty and fragrance and for their form and reliability. And one should not be misled by the popularity of Hybrid Teas and Floribundas ; for they are only two of the 58 classes which make up the sub-divisions of the varieties of cultivated Roses.

THE "SELECT LIST": SHRUB ROSES

GRAHAM S. THOMAS

THE photograph facing page 90 of "Roses: a Select List and Guide to Pruning" shows the Hybrid Musk Vanity displaying some three hundred blooms. The Hybrid Musk Roses do this sort of thing every June and July, after which they produce their big autumnal shoots, each bearing large clusters of flowers. They are, we may say, a step towards the ideal perpetual flowering fragrant shrub Roses which require little pruning and are hardy and vigorous, up to some five feet or so.

Since the Society published its last select list of Roses in 1948, this type of Rose has received more attention, and in these days of stricture, shrubs which flower well and grow well are greatly in demand. It is a good thought that our special flower has filled this need immediately for no other shrubby genus, except perhaps Ceanothus, Hydrangea and Fuchsia, provides so much colour for so long a period and for so little trouble.

To return, Vanity and other favourites such as Felicia, Penelope and Prosperity have had some recent additions to their class, vivid new kinds being Berlin and Bonn and the rich pink Elmshorn. Grandmaster is a rich apricot yellow, somewhat prone to black spot unfortunately; the freshly opened blooms are particularly beautiful before the stamens turn black. These are all new varieties from Kordes, and to them we must now add the brilliant Will Scarlet, a sport from a plant of his called Wilhelm. Will Scarlet received a First Class Trial Ground Certificate in September, 1952. These two make fine shapely bushes up to five feet and the new sport is of a clear scarlet and more fragrant than Wilhelm.

The rugosa Roses have an even longer flowering season and are often in flower by the 20th May. They are trouble-free, dense shrubs up to seven feet high and wide, copiously furnished with handsome wrinkled foliage which turns a clear yellow in the autumn, and the single varieties such as alba and Frau Dagmar Hartopp produce very large red heps. The doubles, Blanc double de Coubert and Roseraie de l'Häy, are among the most fragrant of Roses, their scent carrying well on the air, but they seldom produce heps.

Apart from the rugosas, the perpetual flowering habit has been bred almost entirely from the China Rose, and the carmine-crimson

Great Maidens Blush at Sissinghurst Castle.

SHRUB ROSES IN "THE SELECT LIST"

Frühlingsgold, a new Hybrid Spinosissima raised by Kordes.

YELLOW PINOCCHIO. Floribunda (hyb. poly.)

Raised by E. S. Boerner, of Jackson & Perkins Co. and exhibited by Sam McGredy & Son, Portadown.

First Class Trial Ground Certificate 1951, and Certificate of Merit Show Award 1952.

Fellemberg is one of the strongest growing kinds, making a fairly bushy shrub up to six feet. The single mutabilis grows to a similar height in sheltered conditions and is as remarkable as the new Rose Masquerade in its colouring. The buds are flame red, opening to buff yellow and changing to coppery pink and dark crimson as they age. All the above Roses are suitable for bold plantings and make excellent hedges, with very little pruning. Bourbon Roses, which were the first to show the influx of the China Rose's perpetuality, are now represented by a handful of old stagers which include Mme. Isaac Pereire, perhaps the most powerfully scented of all Roses. This makes an open growing bush and bears very large full blooms of light crimson, in several bursts from June onwards.

The most spectacular of the newer shrub Roses is Nevada, reputed to be a hybrid between an H.T. and Rosa moyesii. This grand shrub has luxuriant light green foliage on arching branches which are studded with the great semi-double flowers in creamy-flesh colour, developing a rich blush-pink in hot weather. It is not particularly fragrant, but has other characteristics to recommend it to all those who wish to plant a perpetual flowering dense shrub of six to seven feet, which needs no pruning except an occasional removal of old wood, has few thorns, and suffers no diseases.

Species or wild Roses have, with few exceptions, one season only of flowering in early summer, but several, such as R. moyesii and its hybrids other than Nevada, produce in August and September magnificent bunches of large scarlet heps, which do much to brighten the garden where eight feet shrubs can be accommodated. It is not often realised that Rosa virginiana can provide as good autumn colour as any shrub, and is very happy running about in sandy or other soils. The yard high thicket of stems bear single pink flowers and red heps. Rosa rubrifolia is unique in foliage colour, too ; the young leaves are of soft purplish grey and the graceful shrub of six feet or so is very attractive when bearing its single pink flowers or clusters of small red heps. These two-season bushes are useful indeed in the garden, bringing to it a breath of the wild and a fresh daintiness that is not found in many other shrubs.

Every year the earliest Roses to flower include the various yellow species among which R. hugonis and its hybrid cantabrigiensis are pre-eminent with arching sprays of single, soft butter-yellow blooms. Unfortunately they do not bear conspicuous fruits. Herr

Kordes has again been successful in this class of Rose, having hybridised the Scotch Rose to produce the light yellow Frühlingsgold. In Surrey this flowers at the end of May at which time no flowering shrub has more beauty. It is very vigorous, up to seven feet, and the four-inch semi-double blooms are lavishly spread over the bush for several weeks. Its sister seedling Frühlingsmorgen is not so vigorous, but has possibly the most exquisite of all single blooms, pink with yellow eye and maroon stamens, and they both bear handsome dark heps in August.

Turning now to Roses for smaller gardens, we have the old Rose groups to consider. These all flower once only, in June and July ; but what a display they make ! Is it not worth having a shrub which provides a hundred blooms during three or four weeks ? The gallicas, or French Roses, for instance, have intensely fragrant double blooms, borne well aloft on bushes up to three or four feet in all colours from blush through pink and crimson to dusky grape-purple. Versicolor (or Rosa Mundi) and Camaieux are two noted striped varieties. Damask Roses and centifolia and Moss Roses are rather more open in habit, but of similar colouring and scent. Many have the habit of producing very double blooms, so packed with petals that those in the centre remain tightly balled giving a " button-centre " from the middle of which a small green eye may be seen. This folding is a style of floral perfection which was much prized in the last century and still excites the admiration of the beholder. Continental raisers gave resounding names like Tour de Malakoff, Chapeau de Napoleon, Nuits de Young, La Ville de Bruxelles, and Cardinal de Richelieu, which contribute not a small part to their enjoyment.

Pruning for these shrub Roses is not an involved task. The old rule for pruning flowering shrubs covers these Roses as well ; those which flower once should have old twiggy wood removed immediately after flowering, unless they are expected to bear heps, when the wood may be removed later. Those flowering through the summer should be pruned in the same way, but not until the spring. As for cultivation, the best is always the cheapest in the long run and thorough preparation by deep digging is advised. The mixture of humus and an annual top dressing in later years, will keep most of them in perfect health, but if a little bone meal or old manure can also be spared it will be found that the blooms are better and last longer.

BUD YOUR OWN PLANTS

BERTRAM PARK

SOONER or later every keen rosarian must try his hand at "budding" his own plants. This does not mean that he becomes a less valuable customer to his nurseryman; on the contrary the Rose lover who is sufficiently interested to master the craft of budding will always be wanting to increase his collection and will always be wanting more and more plants.

Budding is a perfectly simple operation and if carried out on the right lines need present no complexities which any amateur gardener cannot successfully undertake. Obviously the first consideration is the provision of suitable stocks and these should be selected according to the soil conditions in one's garden. A great deal has been said as regards the compatibility of the stock to the scion variety, but it is far more important to have the stocks compatible with the soil and climate. For instance in most parts of North America the Rosa multiflora stock is used; in France multiflora and canina are used in the north and R. odorata in the warm and dry climate of the south. These and other varieties are used in other countries according to the prevailing conditions.

In England the most popular understock is the canina seedling, but it is a very mixed lot and no attempt appears to be made to rogue them; an extraordinary number of sub-varieties may appear, making for unequal growth and "take." Moreover some of the sub-varieties of canina sucker from the roots more readily even than rugosa, which is a cheap stock usually avoided on that account. The so-called R. laxa stock, which is actually a variety of canina, R.×canina froebelii, and is a hybrid of R. alba with R. canina, is extremely even and regular; under good conditions it gives an exceptionally high take, gives vigorous healthy plants, and amongst the thousands which I have used I have never seen a sucker.

On poor and sandy soils there is no doubt that R. multiflora gives the best results, and the thorned variety having prickles singly up the stems and in pairs at the base of the leaf stalks, red when young and black when ripe, is the hardiest and the best; the thornless variety known in the trade as "polyantha simplex" or just "simplex" is unfortunately the one most frequently used. In

BUDDING

The stem with leaves and thorns trimmed

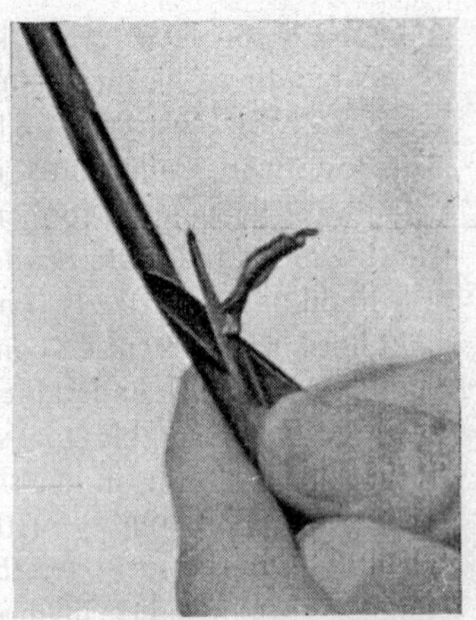

Cutting out the shield

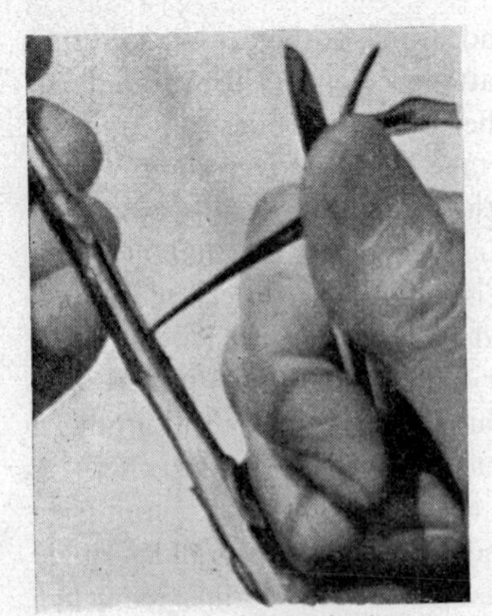

Pulling off the bark

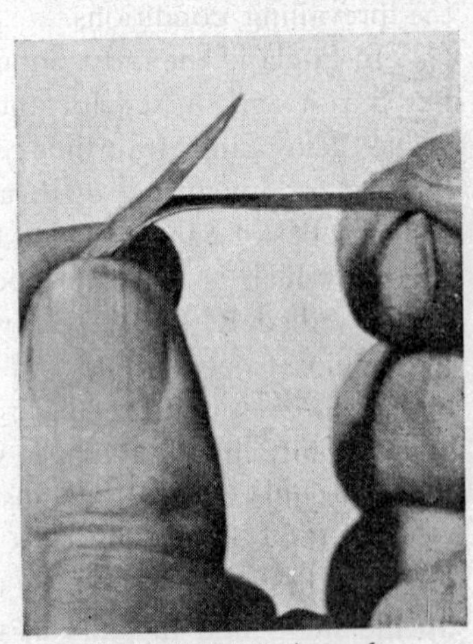

Pulling the bark down from the wood

[The above illustrations and these following are reproduced from "Roses," by Bertram Park, by courtesy of the publishers, Sir Joseph Pittman & Sons.]

September cuttings are taken of the current year's growth about ten inches long, of which the lower cut is made just below an eye and the upper cut just above an eye, the three lower eyes are cut out, and the cuttings inserted two inches apart in sandy soil to root. These will have calloused and rooted well enough the March following to lift and plant in the nursery beds for budding in July and August.

If desired your usual nurseryman will no doubt be able to supply you with some suitable seedling or cutting stocks, and these may be planted in early spring, preferably in a separate plot in the garden, whence they should be transplanted in the year following their first flowering. It is not wise to plant the stocks in the beds where they are to remain permanently, as even in the unlikely event of a 100 per cent. take there are certain to be some inferior plants which will make for inequalities in the bed. Also the roots will be penetrating too deeply, whereas by transplanting and thus trimming the roots these will be kept nearer the surface, which is better for them.

Plant them about ten inches apart and two feet six inches between the rows. If they are seedlings keep the neck, i.e., the part between the root where it forks out and the green shoots above, an inch or so above the level of the ground. If they are rooted cuttings plant the roots as shallow as possible, and both sorts are more conveniently worked if set at a slight slope to the ground. Dry weather in July and August sometimes causes the canina stocks to cease growing, when it is quite useless to try and bud them. One must wait for rain or copious watering with the hose to start them off again, when they can be worked again in a few days. The multiflora stock stands dry weather better, but in wet weather it is inclined to grow too vigorously, it may be restrained by trimming back some of the branches. A stock which grows to much more than half an inch may give unsatisfactory results in that the cut of the heading back will heal over with difficulty and remain open to infection with disease.

Stocks planted in March are ready for budding in July and August. A good quality budding knife should be procured of which the opposite end to the blade is thin and wedge shaped for the purpose of lifting the bark. The blade must be stropped to a razor sharpness on a leather strop or fine emery paper stick. Having chosen the variety to be propagated, select a shoot when the flower is just fading, and before the prickles have dried and hardened ; the leaves are trimmed off leaving about half an inch of the leaf stalk by which

BUDDING

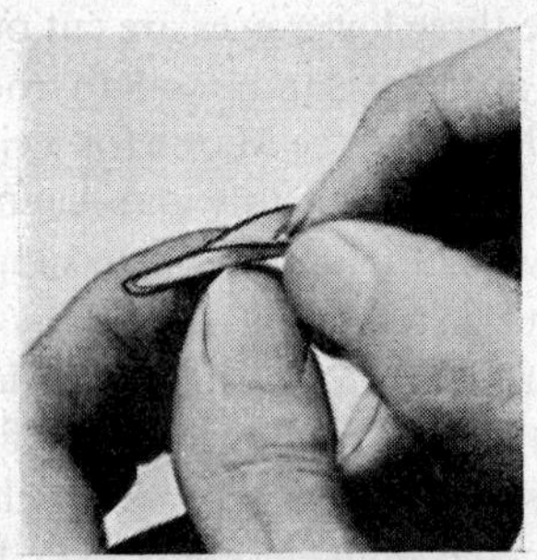

Separating the wood

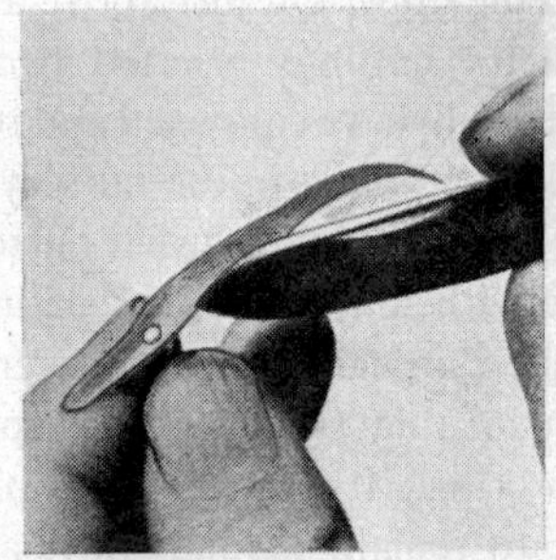

The back of the shield, showing the embryo bud

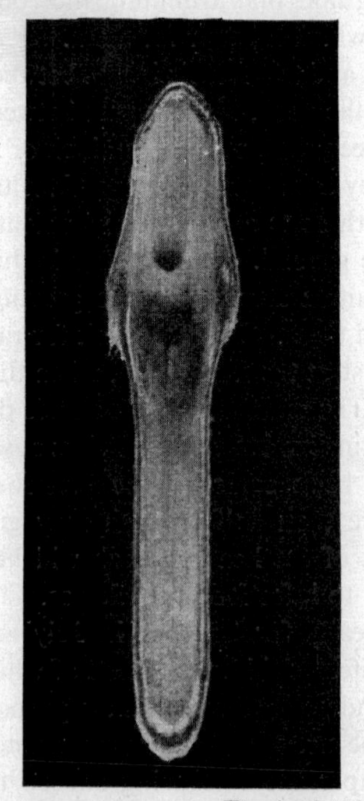

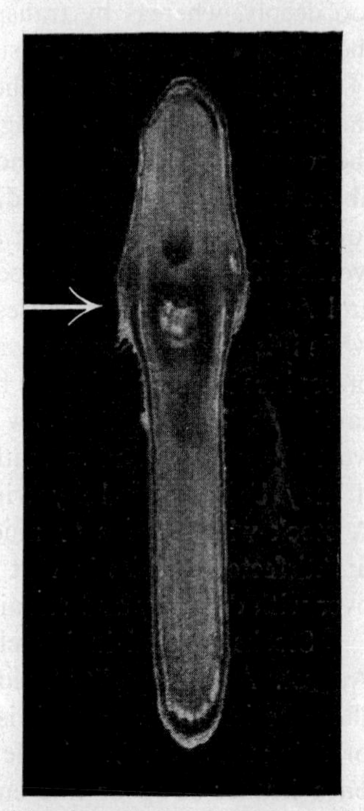

The back of the shield enlarged

Left—Showing the growth torn out.

Right—The growth as it should be, flush with the shield.

to hold the shield. Have some good quality soft raffia cut to a length of 20 inches and stripped to a width of about one-third of an inch.

The professional budder will work down the rows of stocks in a standing position with incredible speed, doing many hundreds a day, but I am getting stiff in the joints as maybe other of our members, and I have to work with one knee on the ground softened, maybe, with a rubber kneeling pad, and my other foot is thrown forward to balance my weight. A flat stick scrapes away the soil from the base of the stock and a rag cleans away any dirt. The whole job should be kept as clean as possible, it is really a surgical operation. An upright cut is made first in the neck of the stock, just deep enough to penetrate the bark but no more, and a cross cut at the top, then with the flat wedge shaped handle of the knife lift up the bark as shown in the illustration. Now without delay take the shoot with the eyes to be used for scions, snap off the prickles and commence to cut out the lowest eye, cut downwards under the eye and upwards half an inch below it, when close down the thumb on to the shield and pull it off with a strip of bark, change the shield to the left hand and pull down the strip of bark to loosen the piece of wood which covers the eye, take hold of this piece of wood and snatch it out with a slight twisting movement. All that now remains is to trim up the shield and it is ready for insertion into the cut in the stock ready for it ; finally tie in firmly with the raffia, two turns below the shield and three above. All this takes long to describe and it may not be very exact but the illustrations should make the whole operation perfectly clear, and when you can work at least 500 a day (I cannot myself) you can call yourself a first-class budder !

Briar standards are budded in exactly the same way, but the eyes are inserted in the laterals, and two or three eyes are used. Rugosa standards are budded in the main stem, and again two or three are put in. The ties on the standards must be cut after about a month, but those on the dwarf stocks will rot off during the winter months and require no more attention.

The next stage, the heading back, is early the next year, in January or February, when the weather is dry and free from frost ; if necessary one must postpone operations until the weather conditions are suitable, but it is not desirable to wait until the sap is rising as then much bleeding will occur. Try and cut the stock as high above the eye as possible, some may already have grown out, and it

BUDDING

The Cut in the lateral of a standard

The shield tied in

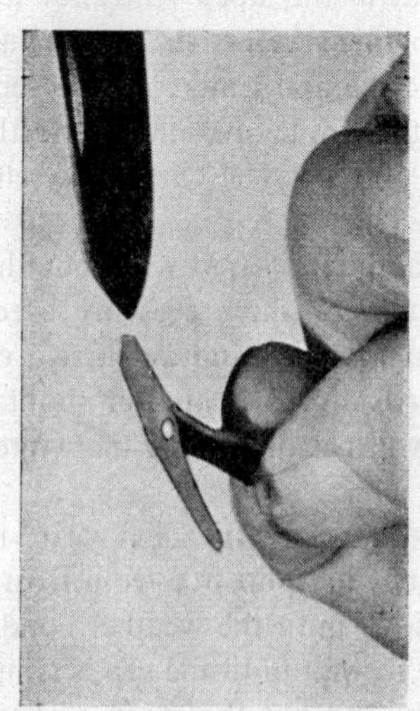

The shield trimmed

The shield inserted and the overlapping piece of bark cut off

is dangerous to cut into the green wood of what was the shield. With cuttings one inch is right but with seedling stocks there may not be an inch to leave, so cut as high as possible. This piece of the stock above the eye will die back in due course and should be trimmed off when the plant is eventually lifted. If the heading back is done close to the bud, I believe that this is when infection from that dread disease canker (Coniothyrium fuckelii) frequently occurs. If there are old plants in the garden, or the same soil has been used before for growing Roses then I think it is desirable to paint the heading back cut with some disinfectant. I have used Bouisol White Oil Emulsion in its concentrated form, straight out of the jar, on a stiff paint brush, and find it satisfactory for the purpose.

Roses budded on to Multiflora stock make a very insecure join the first season, and it is necessary to stake the new growths, tying them first when they are about nine inches high. With other stocks it is not essential but to avoid the risk of damage or blowing out it is just as well also to tie the growths to a short cane. The new plants will flower in June or July and in late October should be lifted and transferred to their permanent quarters.

"*Augerius Busbeckins speaking of the estimation and honour of the Rose, reporteth that the Turks can by no means indure to see the leaves of the Roses fall to the ground, because that some of them have dreamed, that the first or most ancient Rose did spring of the blood of Venus ; and others of the Mahumedans say that it sprang of the sweat of Mahumet.*"

Gerards Herball, 1633.

CARBOHYDRATES AND ROSES

GEORGE A. SWEETSER, WELLESLEY HILLS, MASS.

TO many people the term "carbohydrate" is a mystery. The meaning, however, can be readily understood if we know what carbohydrates are and what they do. Their importance in plant life is great and this article is an effort to explain them so they can be appreciated.

All the food of a plant is manufactured in the leaf. Even the roots are nourished mainly from food produced in the leaf. The food thus manufactured is a form of sugar. Sugar, as everyone knows, is soluble in water. Sap always contains some water. Therefore sugar, being soluble, can be transported over the plant to nourish it and enable it to grow and flower. While this manufacturing process is going on it is difficult for the plant to transport the sugar over the plant as the circulatory system is engaged chiefly in the production of food and not in its distribution.

The manufacture of food goes on only in the daytime under the action of sunlight. Should the plant try to distribute the food at the same time that it is manufacturing it, there might be a "traffic jam," it waits until darkness comes and the manufacturing process ceases before distributing the manufactured food over the plant.

During the daytime the plant changes the sugar to starch and stores it. Almost any housewife knows that starch is not soluble in water. Because of this it is safely stored until the manufacturing process ceases. Both starch and sugar are carbohydrates—combinations of carbon, hydrogen and oxygen, three of the most important substances in plant life.

The plant has the inherent power to change sugar to starch and starch back to sugar at will, a function that is one of the wonders of plant life. Prove it for yourself. Make a test for starch at the end of the day and you will find much of it in the plant if the day has been sunny and the plant has been able to produce the sugar. To prove that this starch has been changed back to sugar and transported over the plant, make another test for starch the next morning. You will find that there is not much starch left where you found it the previous night. This chemical test can easily be made with a little knowledge of chemistry.

The process whereby the plant manufactures its food is as follows : The soil water, with the elements found in the soil dissolved in it, are drawn up into the plant by a process known as osmosis. This process can be explained by the following test : Take two tumblers of water, put sugar or salt in the one, and nothing but water in the other. Put a porous substance (in laboratory tests a pig's bladder is usually used) on top of the tumbler containing the clear water. Now put the two glasses together with the sugar and salt one upside down (not an easy thing to do but it can be done) on top of the glass containing the plain water. There will be a movement of the water from the tumbler containing the clear water into the tumbler containing the sugar or salt. The movement is always from the tumbler containing the lower concentration (in this case the one containing the water only) into the tumbler containing the higher concentration (in this case the water with the starch or sugar) until the concentration in the two tumblers is the same. That is osmosis !

The concentration of the sap of the plant is greater than that of the soil water, thus there is a pull from the soil into the plant. As the sap of the plant contains much water, more or less of which is evaporated into the air as it reaches the leaf, the concentration of the sap is always greater than that of the soil water. Hence there is a continuous pull into the plant.

As the sap reaches the leaf and is distributed through it, the air from the atmosphere enters the leaf through openings on the underside of the leaf called stomata, mingles with the sap and as the sunlight plays upon the leaf it produces chemical action and the food of the plant is produced.

Everyone is familiar with the green colouring matter of the leaf known as chlorophyll, one of the plant pigments. The chlorophyll absorbs the rays of the sun and the chemical action above referred to is produced to make the food of the plant. This process by which a plant grows and is fed is wonderful and almost mysterious.

Thus, these carbohydrates have been referred to as building blocks out of which the plant is made, for the growth and development of a plant depends in no small measure upon the manufacture and utilization of these carbohydrates.

You can see why good foliage is necessary and why spraying or dusting is so needed to preserve that foliage. Another thing is also clear. When you cut off good green wood from your Rose bushes in the spring because you have an idea you can only get good Roses from hard pruned plants, remember you are cutting out some of the building blocks which build up your Rose bush. Of course, if you insist on doing this, then head back your Roses if you prefer, but keep in mind that the green wood contains the substances that give your Rose impetus and start in the spring.

The old idea that you cannot grow fine Roses on tall plants has been pretty well exploded to-day. I have grown fine Roses on tall plants four to six feet tall and anyone can do it if proper cultural practices are followed. In fact, I can show you right in the town in which I live (where Roses bloom in late June) plants four to six feet tall with as fine Roses both in quality and quantity as you will ever see.

On the Pacific coast, due in part to the climate, Roses normally grow four to six feet tall and these tall plants produce beautiful Roses.

Always keep in mind your carbohydrates and preserve those building blocks whenever you can.

¶ LADY MARY FITZWILLIAM.—This famous old Rose is one of the ancestors of over 800 varieties of modern Roses growing in the gardens of the world to-day. Unfortunately it appears to be lost to cultivation. Mr. James Gamble, Trustee of the American Rose Foundation, is most anxious to find a plant or to obtain some budwood, if there is still a plant in existence. If any member should know of a plant the Hon. Editor would be grateful if the member would communicate with him.

LET'S FIRE THE EXPERTS

ROY HENNESSEY, SCAPPOOSE, OREGON

THE Johnsons, like all other people, after they started housekeeping, sooner or later thought their little backyard needed brightening up a bit.

So in a desultory fashion, they talked of putting in some flowers and a garden. About the second spring when Mr. Johnson came home from the office one day, Mrs. Johnson was all enthused, and said, " Herbert, I know what to plant ! " And Herbert dutifully said, " Yes my dear." " Why," said the Mrs., " Roses. Yes, Roses," in a defiant sort of way. Then it was Mr. Johnson's turn to look askance, or even horror stricken. " Why, Darling, have you any idea of all the trouble they are ? Why, Mr. Brown tells me that when he started a Rose bed several years ago, that at the first sight of Roses in his garden he had to put double screens on his windows. When the word got around thru Bugland that there was a new restaurant open, so many bugs came that they could not all get to the new Rose bed at once.

" Then, Tsk, Tsk, the whole Brown family smelled like a drug factory from the sprays and dusts and for weeks it was like that. It was awful."

Some time later after the domestic storm had subsided, they went to the country for a short visit to see some relatives. While wandering about the quiet countryside, they saw a nice looking old garden. As they both like flowers, they stopped and looked.

They saw all manner of flowers growing together in utter confusion. Why, the picture was beautiful. Both felt guilty to admit that they thought so after all the books they had read telling how each flower should be in his little bed just so, and that the Color Experts should pass on whether or not they harmonized. Anyway, they stopped a long time and everything seemed to please them immensely. There were Roses growing and seemingly happy and healthy right among Babys Breath, Zinnias, Delphiniums and at the edges there were Pansies, Lobelias and Sweet Alyssum. They had a feeling of guilt as they came away, for such low taste as to admire what the books had told them was all wrong. Next day they went back that way again (of course by accident) and they stopped. An old couple happened to be in the garden so they asked them how much they had to pay for spray by the barrel. "Spray? Spray? Why, we never spray!"

Then they were told that years ago they planted Roses in beds and everything just as the books said. That seemed to please the bugs no end, as the bugs seemingly want to feed on a straight diet of this or that plant.

Accidently, they went on, they had to plant a lot of annuals in the Rose bed one year to save them. Then the old man got sick and the mixed garden grew on. The plants got big and when they all bloomed together they looked so nice and pretty, as well as seemed to have a lot less bugs on them. So after that they just planted most anything in any place. The bugs seemed rather dazed, not understanding all this or how anyone could mistreat them so as not to have their dinners all in one place, as no self-respecting bug likes to have to hunt for another Rose bush to dine on, and he would never think for a single minute of having a balanced diet.

Apparently our dieticians have never given sufficient publicity to their dietary campaigns. For Bugland continues to have terribly monotonous diets—they just don't know any better. Heavens, it's terrible! Now just think of how much better things would be if our dieticians would start to educate the Rose feeding bugs and start a "Betterment for Bugs" campaign.

Finally the Johnsons decided to buy any plant whenever they wanted to and plant 'em any place and to heck with the Experts as they felt that they could not expect any help from the Federal Dept. of Diets for poor underfed Bugs. For they felt that by following the plan of the old garden they could afford more plants and get hard-hearted about the poor underfed bugs, and it would be the department's fault if some underfed bugs did pass to greener pastures.

One day they talked to an old Horticulturist and found that in field planting he got far better production if all legumes and grasses were grown together. There was far less toxic damage and all were far healthier.

If there is a moral to this article (which I hope there is not) it is that Roses grow, no matter what you do or what care you give. Sometimes I think the care is worse than the abuse.

So please let us not scare the daylight out of the Amateur and let us talk to him of the pleasures and not of the troubles.

ROSES AT HOME

EDNA WHITSITT, SCARSDALE, NEW YORK

ROSES grown in our gardens bring enormous rewards in pleasure as we admire their glowing color and handsome textures. The next step is, of course, to bring some of them inside the home for further enjoyment ; and then comes the thrill and challenge of flower arranging. In its " just right " place in the home, the simplest arrangement can be more heart warming than the show ribbon. The hours of effort that have gone into the flower show display bring the truest pleasure as that practice allows one quickly and easily to make beautiful " flower pictures " at home. Here is the real center of our lives and certainly deserving our best flowers. We are constantly developing greater skill in handling plant material so that the flowers may better express our ideas. But far more important than mere technical skill, there must be an inspiration behind every arrangement for otherwise the whole project is meaningless and wasteful of time and flowers.

Ideas for home arrangements are legion. For instance when one cuts a bouquet of Roses, there must be consciously or otherwise an idea in the back of your head as to where they will look best in the home, whether on the dining room table, in the hall or perhaps on the piano. Flower arrangement is to-day an important part of interior decoration. The gardener-homemaker orders her Roses with an eye to the interior color scheme as well as the outdoor garden plan. Most of us are endlessly collecting here and there, from the finest stores to the junk shops, containers that will augment our flowers and beautify our homes. The most useful container is apt to be the neutral colored one ; for like the " basic dress " it goes with everything. A container for flowers must be of good design and the correct selection plays an important role in the success of our ideas. More often than not it dictates or at least suggests the design plan of the arrangement.

Roses coöperate splendidly with the flower arrangers, no weak floppy stems here, the foliage has interesting form and a glossy elegance of texture. The color range is in itself an inspiration moving from the palest tints to the dark rich shades of red. There is the gay coral of Fashion and the subtle cherry red of Vogue, beautiful variations in the yellows and oranges and the clean purity of the white Roses.

But back to practical concerns. There are many places in the home for our Roses and whether the decoration is formal or more casual, the Roses are appropriate. Gone, I hope, is the belief that only crystal or silver can serve as a container for Roses. Copper, pewter, wood, porcelain, alabaster and pottery are usable too and usually a great deal more fun. The style of the room and the color, design and texture of the container will help decide which vase to use.

As family and guest come and go the front hall is the first and last place they see. Here the visitor is welcomed, and certainly is a place worthy of the homemaker's best talents. What better opportunity to convey the mood of the home ? Since halls are apt to have a table or chest holding a lamp, a low bowl is an excellent choice if the lamp is tall, thereby avoiding competition in heighths. When the lamp is lit, the low placed flowers are spot-lighted by the glow falling into the arrangement ; which might happily have a low crescent as its design plan. And as halls are often darker than other rooms select light bright Roses, saving the darker more subtle colors for sunnier locations.

Living rooms suggest a number of spots where an arrangement will be a successful adjunct to interior decoration. The piano calls for the large important arrangement. Heighth is usually no problem so the large urn and the heavier flowers may be used effectively, and here the large formal triangle design is often pleasant. Since the fireplace is the focal point of the room, the mantel clamors for flowers. Its formal symmetry may suggest a pair of arrangements on either side of a picture or mirror. But be certain that these vases are in line with the pilasters so as to preserve the calm and dignity of the ensemble.

Coffee tables occupy an attention-commanding location. The arrangement must be so placed and scaled as to leave adequate space for coffee or cocktail service. Remember that this is a piece of furniture with a definite use and must not be smothered with a too large arrangement. It will be most satisfying if kept low and designed to be " looked down into." Little occasional tables can be made more beautiful by a small bouquet but again there must be no crowding of the lamp, the ash tray, and the evening paper.

y courtesy] [Jackson & Perkins Co., New York

Ma Perkins Rose arranged in a blue Bristol vase by Edna Whitsitt.

By courtesy] *[Jackson & Perkins Co., New York*

Coral Dawn Climber arranged by Edna Whitsitt.

Dining room tables need flowers most of all, and every homemaker, whether flower arranger or not, occasionally fixes flowers for the dining room. Reams have been written about the necessity of relating the arrangements, the china, glassware, and the linen, both as to color and texture. For example the informal pottery plates and the heavy woven mats will not be well related to a porcelain or silver urn filled with a formal arrangement, while a pewter or pottery container less formally handled will be much more pleasing. Table arrangements obviously receive the closest scrutiny. Wash all foliage carefully to remove any traces of dirt or spray and beware of the " bug chewed leaf." Be a good arrangement housekeeper too. And do sit as you make the dining table arrangement for the result must be low enough or airy enough so the family and guests can be a conversational unit without having to peer around an overpowering centerpiece.

Formerly it might have seemed almost impolite to a Rose to consider it as material for an arrangement in the kitchen. But the cheery little Geranium Red with its open bloom both looking and smelling like a geranium is much at home in a wood mortar or bowl on the kitchen window sill. Its perfume and gay color will shorten kitchen hours.

Whether your Rose bushes are numbered by the hundreds or a quickly counted few there are usually enough to bring some inside. When only a few are available, a small grouping can be used as the focal point in an arrangement with evergreen or house plant foliage as the line material. Use your Roses to bring charm and color into your home and the rewarding joy of creating beautiful flower pictures.

"*The fruit* (*of the briar Rose*) *when it is ripe maketh most pleasant meats and banquishing dishes, as tarts and such like ; the making thereof I commit to the cunning cooke, and teeth to eat them in the rich mans mouth.*"

Gerards Herbal, 1633.

A VISITOR FROM SOUTH AFRICA

J. LIEBSON, Pretoria.

ONE Tuesday afternoon early in August Mr. Bertram Park met me at Stanmore Station and took me in his car to the National Rose Society's Trial Grounds at Oaklands. This visit was the fulfilment of a prospect which had been in my mind during my travels on the Continent. As I moved from country to country, I was in a state of anticipation and exhilaration, I was receptive to everything I saw and experienced, impressions were laid thick one upon the other ; and yet I knew that something was awaiting me on my return to England which in its simple way would evoke a more intimate response.

It was not one of the visitors' days when, I was told, as many as five hundred people come to the grounds. As I was off home again in a day or two to South Africa I was granted a special permit. I had the freedom of moving at my leisure from one bush to the next, from one bed to another, always with Mr. Park or Mr. Baines, the Trial Ground Superintendent, at my side, to give me information, to point out special features of interest, to give my enquiries direction when it was needed. The thought constantly came to my mind that here was the ground where some new Rose I was seeing had passed, or would pass, the test so important for its disposal in its myriads all over the Commonwealth and in many other parts of the world besides. And it was a rigorous test. On that perfect day, the superficial eye would only have seen the beauty of the place and its surroundings. But the conditions were as hard as they could be within reason. There were no windbreaks. The ground was wide open to the elements. The soil was of a yellow, tough, clayey composition which cultivation could not disguise. And then as a South African I was surprised to hear (Mr. Park was so emphatic that I almost felt abashed at my question) that the plants were never watered. But that I understood was not unusual treatment, it was the rule. Here in South Africa where (with the exception of the coastal areas) the summer rains are apt to be of a torrential nature, where after a heavy shower the sky is as clear and the sun shines as hotly as ever and weeks may elapse between rains, no garden could exist without the hosepipe ; and my Roses are heavily watered at least once a week, a scraping of the surface soil to provide a slight mulch frequently being resorted to the day after as a further means to conserve the moisture.

On the first Sunday of every July the Pretoria Horticultural Society provides a public Rose pruning demonstration, and for a great number of years it has been my job to carry out this function. When, therefore, Mr. Park took me to the beds where different systems of pruning are being tested, I realised that something important to me would be disclosed and I hoped to find confirmation of my views. I saw enough to satisfy me that the conviction which had gradually been forming in my mind over the years was justified—that Roses respond best to long pruning.

In my ignorant days I accepted blindly what I saw. If a Rose bed had suffered a savage assault in a park, or by an itinerant "expert" pruner in some private garden, I felt that was right. The very fact that several feet of growth had been reduced to nothingness seemed to justify the process. But with the passage of time it was brought home to me that one must pay regard to "balance" in growth—that good pruning in the main really consisted of elimination and not so much of reduction of growth, and that the root system required to support a large bush was excessive for a smaller plant, so that the body of roots shrank in sympathy with the reduction of the plant. In effect, a heavily pruned bush was not something which promised soon to be or to exceed what it had been before—it had become a dwarfed plant with roots which would shrink to its lesser requirements. A weaker plant had taken the place of the previous plant.

And here at the Trial Grounds there were the "hard-pruning," the "medium-pruning" and the "light-pruning" beds. There could be no doubt that the bushes in the last were the best and those which had been subjected to hard pruning the worst. From the plants which had been light-pruned were emerging those fat basal shoots which are the promise of vigorous growth, and these were much rarer in the other two beds. And further confirmation of the system which merely requires the slightest reduction of strong growth accompanied by the elimination of exhausted and dead wood, weakly twigs and such stems as are obviously superfluous or in the way, was found in Mr. Park's statement that in the first great flush of the season's flowering, the quality of the blooms from the long-pruned bushes were as good as, if not better than, from the bushes which had been more heavily pruned.

What I saw in the Trial Grounds indicated that the trend towards Roses of the floribunda character has gained a great impetus, and I consider this regrettable. I should say that fifty per cent. of the plants were of that type. I understand they are in great demand for public gardens and for bedding generally. But whilst they are lovely subjects and spectacular in the mass, the development of varieties of the hybrid tea type should not be made to suffer because of this new fashion. There can be no question which is the true emblem of the Rose world. It is the one large bloom rising in all its majesty and beauty on its single stem and proudly supported on its strong pedicel, slowly unfolding in form and colour from bud to fully developed flower. I saw one crimson head of bloom and I could hardly credit my eyes. It was a tightly packed pyramidal mass of flower, anything up to a foot and a half high and almost a foot in width. From a distance it looked like a vast head of phlox decussata. It was a magnificent specimen of hybrid polyantha but I could not call it beautiful. The intrinsic Rose was lost in it. (Tantau's Delight.—*Ed.*)

But there were many floribundas carrying their flowers in loose sprays of large blooms and these were lovely. There was one bush which although it appeared to me to be rather of the floribunda habit I thought was one of the finest Roses in the Trial Grounds. It had already been awarded a First Class Certificate. Its good-sized blooms, well spaced apart, were of a perfect camellia shape and of an extraordinary colouring which I can only inadequately describe as sealing wax red. It stood in the third year testing bed, some yards from Independence, which I understood was one of its parents, the other being Crimson King. It was still unnamed and bore the number 363.

I would have needed much more time amongst the Roses at the Trial Grounds to make up my mind which most impressed me. (I realised, of course, that I was seeing them at a time when they were not at their best.) But I do remember particularly Tzigane, George Sands, Independence, Border King, William Harvey, Commonwealth, Eden Rose, Dr. Debat, Marcel Gret, Mme. Yves Latieule, Symphonie, Cocorico, and a large bush—a hybrid musk bearing the name of Berlin.

ROSES IN NEW ZEALAND

C. V. HOLYOAKE,
Immediate Past-President, National Rose Society of New Zealand

EVEN though we live "at the other end of the earth" the Rose Annual is eagerly looked forward to each year for it is recognised locally as the most authoritative and up-to-date publication on Rose matters. It is with some trepidation, therefore, that I respond to your invitation to contribute to its pages. I will try to give you a picture of the background of Roses in this Dominion.

Our soils are like yours in that they vary greatly from place to place ; the main difference is that they have been cultivated for less than 100 years and are, therefore, comparatively virgin. The climate is different but you will have some idea if you imagine a land similar in breadth to your own but in latitudes stretching for 1,000 miles from the South of England to the Madeira Islands. We have no Gulf Stream, however, and the climate in our coldest districts is similar to that in Southern Scotland.

The colder climates produce Roses of more substance and deeper colour and, in fact, the variation is so great that experienced rosarians from the sub-tropical north have difficulty in recognizing some varieties in the south and vice versa. I have seen our President Emeritus, Frank Penn (an exhibitor of over 50 years' standing), stumped when visiting far from home.

In the warmer districts growth is much more abundant, but rust, black spot and green fly also do better. The rainfall is fairly regular in most districts but this is a mixed blessing in the north (your south) because of the accompanying humidity which encourages blights and insect pests. It is rather paradoxical, therefore, that in spite of the handicaps, there are more Rose enthusiasts in the north than in the south.

Membership of the New Zealand Rose Society stands at approximately 3,000, or one for every 700 of the population. Members are grouped into 17 District Rose Societies and the National Rose Society of New Zealand acts as the central co-ordinating body. Policy matters are decided at the Annual Meeting of the National Society which is comprised of delegates from the District Societies. An Executive Committee and various sub-Committees look after the business side of the Headquarters organization in between times. The Annual Meeting is held in the winter (June) and the only other really National gathering is in the show season (November) when a Convention of approximately one week's duration is held in conjunction with the National Show. This dual event is organized by different District Societies each year with the help of National Headquarters and is growing in popularity. Members learn more about Roses at a Convention than at an Annual Meeting for the Convention activities include visits to the outstanding gardens in the area.

Each District Society is really self-governing. There is uniformity in the judging rules for shows and in other matters in which standardization is desirable, but in many respects their activities differ according to local circumstances. Where a Horticultural Society provides facilities for shows, the local Rose Society usually supports them but in other cases the Rose Societies hold their own shows. In quite a number of exhibitions the Rose classes attract from 500 to 700 entries and a surprising improvement in the general exhibition standard has resulted since the District Societies were first formed in 1945, 1946 and 1947. Other district activities include Rose pruning demonstrations, lectures, the promotion of civic Rose gardens, garden competitions, etc.

Plank number one in our policy is "to implant Roses in the hearts and gardens of the people." We believe that it is more important to grow Roses than to show Roses and our shows are designed to educate people to grow better Roses rather than as a battle-field for the expert exhibitors. An illustration of this point is the fact that even in classes for exhibition Roses we prohibit the use of any artificial aid (wiring or extra stems) to support the blooms, and staging in boxes is practically unknown. Needless to say, there are many veteran exhibitors and they are very valuable to us, but we concern ourselves most with encouraging the tyros for we believe that if we can develop interest in the home and garden we are helping to make better citizens.

Public Rose gardens and wayside Rose plots are becoming quite a feature of our land and it gives one quite a thrill to come unexpectedly upon a new formal civic Rose garden or a roadside plot and to know that members of our Society have been at work.

Our Governor-General, Lord Freyberg, mentioned this fact recently when opening one of our shows.

It has been my pleasure to meet officers and members of all of our District Societies and I can testify that the Rose is a means of bringing together men of all walks of life and of all creeds, and uniting them in fellowship and in a love of the beautiful. The Rose is truly cosmopolitan and breaks down all barriers.

THE GARDENER'S MISTRESS

Have you ever toiled with all your strength and mind
 And precious time, to make your Rose trees grow,
Only, uncultivated and unloved, to find
 The next-door bushes make a braver show ?
Yes. The Rose is of the contrary kind.

And have you seen her stricken with a blight,
 Black spot, and Rust, and every kind of pest,
And still, miraculously, over-night,
 Lifting her head, and giving of her best
Drawn from the muck and sweat for your delight ?

When you're a gardener, you can't be proud,
 Knowing, where weather frowns, all work is vain,
Yet, partners with Providence, you brag aloud
 To see your outlay flooding back again
A thousand-fold, where glowing beauties crowd.

K. S.

PURPLE SPOTTING OF ROSE LEAVES

DURING the past season we have had numerous complaints of defoliation of Rose plants in spraying against Black Spot. In every case on investigation, it was found that there had actually been no Black Spot present, the defoliation being due to other causes. In one case the member had used Copper Oil Emulsion Spray and then " to make quite sure " had sprayed again, using another proprietary preparation. This unfortunately contained a form of organic sulphur, which, reacting with the previous spray, had disastrous results on the plants.

Never mix sprays unless it is known that they are compatible.

Moreover it was ascertained that this member lived in an industrial area, with many factory chimneys in the vicinity; it was, therefore, extremely improbable that there was any disease at all in his garden.

Do not spray unnecessarily.

There is a " Purple Spotting " sometimes evident on Rose leaves which must not be confused with Black Spot, and when this occurs it is a symptom that the soil is lacking in some essential element, with resultant nutrient deficiency. In such cases the plant is physiologically unbalanced, it is not in a healthy condition, and the foliage may then be damaged by *any* spray.

The cure is better cultivation and the provision of organic manures, garden compost, strawy farmyard or stable dung, fish guano and so on.

The photographs and captions on adjoining pages will assist the identification of " Black Spot." They have very kindly been provided by Miss Wilson, plant pathologist, on behalf of Boots Pure Drug Co., Ltd., from their research station at Lenton, Nottingham.

B. P.

Photograph illustrating true Black Spot of Rose caused by the fungus Actinonema Rosae (Lib). Fr.

A " close-up " of two leaflets, showing the typical " fringed " appearance of the younger spots which is such a valuable diagnostic character.

Rose Powdery Mildew Spotting.

[*Photographs by courtesy of the Research Department of Boots Pure Drug Co., Ltd.*

Showing various stages of the Rose Powdery Mildew caused by the fungus Sphaerotheca pannosa (Waller) Lév. The leaves on the left show the small raised purple spots, a common effect of this mildew.

Photograph illustrating true Black Spot of Rose caused by the fungus Actinonema Rosae (Lib.) Fr.

[*Photograph by courtesy of the Research Department of Boots Pure Drug Co., Ltd.*

Showing typical forms of the Spot in various stages. The " fringed " edge of the spot is clearly seen, particularly on the leaf in the left-hand bottom corner.

Photograph illustrating PURPLE SPOTTING due to various causes and often mistaken for Black Spot.

[Photograph by courtesy of the Research Department of Boots Pure Drug Co., Ltd.

Showing various forms of **Purple Spotting,** none of which is true Black Spot. These purple discolorations are usually symptoms of physiological disorders, and though the exact causes are still obscure, evidence suggests that the major factors are unsuitable soil conditions and nutritional deficiencies. Susceptibility to purple spotting varies very much with variety.

Mr. Oliver Mee in his Cheshire garden with a bed of Mrs. Sam McGredy Roses, photographed on July 12, 1934.

ECONOMICAL LONG TERM PLANNING IN THE ROSE GARDEN.

The same bed of Roses and the same plants, none has been replaced, photographed in July, 1952, over 20 years after planting.

THE SUMMER ROSE SHOW

By ROY HAY

THIS was the finest summer Rose Show that I have seen since the war. In point of quality it might be that it was the finest summer Show that we have ever had, but memory is a fickle thing and so many distractions have intervened since the carefree days when we used to wander through the tents in Chelsea Hospital gardens, that I would not care to make any comparisons.

Nevertheless, even a hardened critic of Shows—and I see an average of about three a week—could not fail to be moved by the long avenue of nurserymen's groups, a solid wall of glorious colour, that burst upon our line of vision as we entered the hall. I suppose that the judges could have found a fault with Messrs. R. Harkness and Co.'s exhibit, which won the Queen Mary's Cup and Trophy and also a Gold Medal. I could find none. It was a clean bold group which was beautiful whichever way you looked at it. The cascading effect they achieved with their bowls of superb blooms was not equalled by any other exhibitor in my estimation. In this exhibit Charles Mallerin justified itself as a Rose to look at as well as a Rose to smell. The dainty hybrid musk variety Prosperity was another that took my fancy, but there were so many desirable varieties that a selection is invidious. The Norman Rogers Cup went to Messrs. A. J. Meredith and Son, and here again quality of blooms must have influenced the judges. I found the arrangement pleasing but orthodox. On the other hand, Messrs. C. Gregory and Son, Ltd., in their Coronation Trophy display on island tabling, struck a new line, and their bowls on angled arms gave the impression of lightness at the same time presenting to the visitor a bewildering selection of varieties and a vast array of blooms.

I assume, in my simplicity, that the idea of the exhibitor in these classes is to pack in as many varieties as possible, to use as many blooms as necessary to create a lavish and breath-taking effect, and generally to create as imposing an exhibit as possible within a limited space. I suppose that by now practically every possible arrangement has been tried, and it would be interesting to know how the different exhibits compare for numbers of blooms and numbers of varieties. Next year, if I can persuade my secretary to take on the job, I will have a count made of some of the different styles of exhibits, and see where we get !

I see from my notes that my summing up of the impressions provided by the trade groups included " do not like pseudo beds " which, being translated, means that these imitation Rose beds where the vases are hidden by moss or turf, and cut blooms are jammed in to give an impression of a Rose bed somehow fail to achieve the desired effect. Another note reads, " combination of cascading pillars and bowls of Roses, or even the exhibits composed entirely of cascading effect—very attractive." For what they are worth, those were the impressions. After having walked round the hall several times, and stood back to admire the glorious bank of colour, I amused myself by jotting down the names of varieties whose colouring stood out really brilliantly among the hundreds on view. Again, for what they are worth, here are those that seemed most striking for colour in the hall : Charles Mallerin (strangely enough), The Doctor, McGredy's Yellow, Mrs. Sam McGredy, Ena Harkness, McGredy's Sunset, Hector Deane, Peace, Mrs. A. R. Barraclough, and Spek's Yellow, among the Hybrid Tea varieties, and Frensham, Fashion and Goldilocks among the Hybrid Polyantha Roses.

After these reflections, not very profound, perhaps, I spent an hour admiring the amateur exhibits in the old hall. Mr. M. L. Kemp, of Halstead, certainly made the running hot in his race to win the Courtney Page Cup. His box of twelve blooms was exceptionally good, and his six vases of blooms in the H. R. Darlington Cup class were also unusually fine, especially his blooms of Crimson Glory, Mrs. Foley Hobbs, and Mrs. C. Lamplough. I liked, too, his bloom of Sam McGredy in the Lindsell Cup class. Mr. Kemp was certainly a worthy amateur champion. Mr. F. Bridgstock, of Kettering, must also have been a happy man in the knowledge that his bowl of twelve different Roses was so far ahead of his competitors. The Edward Mawley Memorial Medal for the highest aggregate of points in the section for amateurs growing their Roses without assistance was deservedly won by Mr. Bridgstock with his polished exhibits.

After these stalwarts the running became less hectic. Mr. E. Royalton Kisch certainly showed a fine box of twelve specimen blooms in the Edward Mawley Challenge Cup class, and his bloom of Ena Harkness in the six-bloom box class was probably his best flower of all. Mr. G. D. Burch, however, showed some very fine Roses, and his bloom of Leni Neuss in the six specimen bloom class in Division B was very fine.

Mr. R. White, of Aylesbury, a powerful prize winner, certainly had some fine blooms of Rex Anderson in the class for six specimen blooms of one variety. I know that it is bad form to criticise the judges, but when I saw this class, only a few minutes after the judges had left, I must say that I preferred the second Prize exhibit of Peace, but then I am prejudiced in favour of this superb variety.

Perhaps the judges were tired of seeing Peace, as I am sure they must have been of Frensham in the class for a bowl of six stems of Hybrid Polyantha varieties. Maybe with so many fine new varieties in this section coming to the fore, Frensham will have to take a back seat, but it is unlikely that it will disappear altogether yet.

It is becoming increasingly obvious that the Rose is a sufficiently beautiful flower in its own right, not to need the artifice of the modern " line arrangement " to make it attractive as a cut flower. In the artistic class, there were several bowls in the upswept modern style, but several of us who examined the entries very carefully came to the conclusion that we preferred the old style. We even persuaded Julia Clements to agree with us that the Rose does not lend itself to line arrangement.

There was a tendency this year to break new ground in the table decoration classes. Mrs. D. Thorn's entry of Picture in a simple vase with three sprays laid flat in holders was original and very attractive, but on the whole one came away with the feeling that it should be possible to make a break with the traditional and achieve something really striking with these table decorations. This argument goes on interminably, and one is tempted to suggest that one year it might be interesting to ask a professional flower arranger to submit a demonstration piece, not for competition. We might then find out what all the argument is about. There seems to be a good deal of chance about the artistic classes, because Mrs. Temple Twining's table decoration of old fashioned Roses just did not come off. We remember vividly some of her previous efforts with old fashioned Roses, and were disappointed with her effort this time. It seems that the simple self-colours, such as Miss Gwen Woollard's lovely table of yellow Roses, are the best in the long run. At least the competitors in the artistic classes have now given up the footling little corner vases on the tables, which only get knocked over and add very little to the general effect.

The metropolitan classes were better than in 1951, in fact most of the entries were of very high quality. The novices, as usual, showed their flowers mostly too fully opened, although Mr. Herbert Sumner, of Romford, had blooms of Red Ensign and Crimson Glory which your humble scribe would have been proud to show at our local exhibition.

And so there were more Roses, more entries in the classes, and certainly more people than we have seen at any Rose show since the war. Thank goodness I have the privilege of a Press ticket, and do not have to fight my way round the exhibits. What happens when the Society reaches the fifty thousand mark, I leave to the President and Council to worry about.

PRIZE WINNERS—GREAT SUMMER SHOW, 1952.

Class

NURSERYMEN

1. **H. M. Queen Mary's Challenge Cup and Championship Trophy.** A representative group, 20-ft. by 4-ft. 1, R. Harkness and Co., 2, R. Tucker and Son; 3, F. Cant and Co.; E. W. Stedman, Ltd.; John Mattock.
2. **The Norman Rogers Challenge Cup.** A representative group, 10-ft. by 4-ft. 1, A. J. Meredith and Son; 2, F. Carter; 3, Cramphorn's Nurseries.
3. **The Coronation Trophy.** Group on island tabling, 12-ft. by 8-ft. 1, C. Gregory and Sons, Ltd.; 2, B. R. Cant and Sons, Ltd.; 3, Wheatcroft Bros., Ltd.; 4, W. Lowe and Son, Ltd.
4. **The China Trophy.** 24 Distinct varieties on tabling 12-ft. by 6-ft. 1, J. Townsend and Son; 2. F. Cant and Co.
5. **Thirty stems** of any one variety sent out between 1st June, 1947, and 31st December, 1951, staged in bowl not exceeding 12-in. in diameter. 1, S. Eacott, 2, Cramphorn's Nurseries; 3, S. Treseder and Son.
6. **The John Hart Memorial Cup.** Forty-eight blooms, distinct varieties. 1, R. Harkness and Co; 2, Clifford Longley (Roses) Ltd.; 3, F. Cant and Co.
7. **The Kilbee Stuart Memorial Cup.** Twenty-four blooms, distinct varieties. 1, F. Cant and Co.; 2, Jarman and Co.; 3, Clifford Longley (Roses) Ltd.
8. **Twelve Blooms,** distinct varieties sent out between 1st June, 1947, and 31st December, 1951. 1, Clifford Longley (Roses) Ltd.; R. Harkness and Co.
9. **The Lewis Levy Memorial Cup.** Three Baskets of Hybrid Polyanthas 1, R. Harkness and Co.; 2, F. Cant and Co.; 3, R. M. Tooke; 4, E. W. Stedman, Ltd.
10. **Two Baskets of Polyantha Roses.** 1, G. Longley and Son; 2, J. Townsend and Son; 3, F. Cant and Co.
11. **Three Baskets of Cut Roses.** 1, S. Treseder and Son.
12. **The A. C. Turner Challenge Cup.** Fifteen vases, distinct. 1, S. Treseder and Son; 2, J. Townsend and Sons, 3 R. M. Tooke.
13. **Dinner Table Decoration.** 1, Mrs. Tisdall.
14. **Bowl Decoratively Arranged.** 1, Mrs. C. A. Tisdall; 2, F. Carter; 3, Denys Lawrence; 4, H. Drew.
15. **Vase Decoratively Arranged.** 1, Mrs. C. A. Tisdall; 2, Denys Lawrence; 3, Alan Gibbs; 4, F. Carter.

AMATEUR—Open Classes

18. **Bowl of 18 stems.** 1. R. White; 2, Miss H. M. Boyer, 3, W. J. Northfield.
19. **Bowl of 12 stems.** 1, R. White; 2, A. N. Warren; 3, W. J. Northfield.
20. **Three vases Polyantha or Hybrid Polyantha,** distinct. 1, A. N. Warren; 2, L. P. Roberts; 3, R. White; 4, J. R. Colyer.
21. **One Bowl Polyantha or Hybrid Polyantha,** 12 stems, one variety. 1, A. N. Warren; 2, R. White; 3, J. R. Colyer.
22. **The S. W. Burgess Memorial Cup.** Six vases decorative Roses. 1, E. M. Allen; 2, W. J. Northfield; 3, R. White.
23. **The Edward Mawley Challenge Cup.** Box of 12 specimen blooms. 1, E. Royalton Kisch; 2, R. White; 3, W. J. Northfield; 4, W. H. J. Sansum.
24. **Box of Six Specimen Blooms,** two of each. 1, E. Royalton Kisch; 2, A. N. Warren; 3, R. White; 4, W. J. Northfield.
25. **Box of Six Specimen Blooms,** one variety. 1, R. White; 2, Mrs. K. Konig; 3, W. J. Northfield; 4, A. N. Warren.
26. **Two Vases Specimen Blooms.** 1, R. White; 2, E. Royalton Kisch; 3, C. C. Williamson; 4, L. P. Roberts.

26a. **The Lindsell Cup.** Box of 24 specimen blooms. 1, M. L. Kemp, 2, R. White; 3, W. J. Northfield.

Amateurs who grow and stage without assistance

27. **Bowl of 18 stems.** 1, Miss H. M. Boyer.

28. **Bowl of 12 stems.** 1, A. W. J. Green; 2, A. Norman.
29. **Three Vases Polyantha or Hybrid Polyantha,** distinct. 1, L. A. Anstiss; 2, M. L. Kemp; 3, H. C. Wilson; 4, A. Norman.
30. **Bowl of Polyantha or Hybrid Polyantha Roses,** 12 stems. 1, M. L. Kemp; 2, E. Royalton Kisch; 3, A. Norman.
31. **The H. R. Darlington Memorial Cup,** six vases. 1, M. L. Kemp; 2, A. Norman.
32. **The Nicholson Challenge Cup.** Box 12 distinct. 1, M. L. Kemp; 2, G. D. Burch; 3, A. Norman.
33. **The Brayfort Challenge Cup.** Box six distinct. 1, L. A. Anstiss; 2, E. Royalton Kisch; 3, G. D. Burch.
34. **Box of Six,** three distinct varieties. 1, M. L. Kemp; 2, L. A. Anstiss; 3, G. D. Burch.
35. **Box of Six,** one variety. 1, G. D. Burch; 2, L. A. Anstiss; 3, M. L. Kemp; 4 W. H. J. Sansum.
36. **Two Vases,** three blooms in each. 1, L. A. Anstiss.

Restricted to growers of not more than 500 trees who grow and stage without assistance

37. **One Bowl,** 12 stems. 1, T. Bridgstock; 2, E. E. Gatward; 3, H. G. Clacy.
38. **One Bowl Hybrid Polyantha or Polyantha Roses,** nine stems. 1, C. Somerset; 2, E. E. Gatward; 3, H. C. Wilson; 4, D. Pope.
39. **Four Vases,** distinct varieties in each. 1, T. Bridgstock; 2, H. C. Wilson; 3, Mrs. E. Toogood.
40. **The Sam McGredy Challenge Cup.** Box of six specimen blooms. 1, C. Sales, 2, A. E. Barton; 3, F. E. Timbrell; 4, E. E. Gatward.
41. **The Mrs. Foley Hobbs Memorial Prize.** Box of six blooms. 1, W. C. Thorn; 2, A. E. Barton; 3, C. F. Warren; 4, J. E. Eld.
42. **Two Vases Specimen Blooms.** 1, A. E. Barton; 2, A. Cobley; 3, T. Bridgstock; 4, E. E. Gatward.
43. **One Vase Six Specimen Blooms.** 1, T. Bridgstock, 2, Miss A. M. Aldous; 3, A. E. Barton; 4, J. E. Eld.

Restricted to growers of not more than 250 trees who grow and stage without assistance

44. **One Bowl,** twelve stems. 1, J. F. Harkness; 2, E. H. Pollitt; 3, G. Walters; 4, P. H. Hall.
45. **Three Vases,** four stems. 1, A. T. Barnes; 2, J. F. Harkness; 3, Miss H. I. Port; 4, Mrs. S. Cowen.
46. **One Bowl Hybrid Polyantha or Polyantha,** six stems. 1, A. T. Barnes; 2, J. F. Harkness; 3, C. Somerset; 4, M. H. Bristow.
47. **One Bowl Hybrid Polyantha or Polyantha,** six stems, one variety. 1, J. F. Harkness; 2, M. H. Bristow; 3, C. M. Lister; 4, Mrs. S. Cowen.
48. **Box of Six Specimen Blooms.** 1, Mrs. MacGeorge; 2, J. E. Wiseman; 3, E. L. Boddington; 4, Miss E. Pickering.
49. **Vase Three Specimen Blooms.** 1, Mrs. MacGeorge; 2, E. H. Pollitt; 3, J. E. Wiseman.
50. **Vase Three Specimen Blooms.** 1, J. E. Wiseman; 2, Mrs. MacGeorge; 3, J. F. Harkness.

Metropolitan Classes

51. **Bowl of Decorative Roses,** twelve stems. 1, L. Hollis; 2, H. C. Wilson; 3, J. N. Harvie.
52. **The Gardeners' Company Challenge Cup.** Box six specimen blooms. 1, J. N. Harvie, 2, L. Hollis; 3, N. A. Gibson.
53. **One Vase Six Specimen Blooms.** 1, H. C. Wilson; 2, J. Hines; 3, N. A. Gibson; 4, D. L. Flexman.

Restricted to growers of not more than 150 trees who grow and stage without assistance

54. **One Vase,** Six stems, 1, W. G. H. Cates; 2, P. W. Jakeman; 3, A. H. Arnold; 4, Mrs. M. Pearce.
55. **The Charles Rigg Cup.** Box of six specimen blooms. 1, P. W. Jakeman; 2, J. R. Hayley; 3, Miss P. M. Brown.
56. **Vase Six Specimen Blooms.** 1, Miss B. Somerset; 2, G. R. Mack; 3, B. W. W. Sampson.
57. **Vase Three Specimen Blooms,** distinct. 1, W. G. H. Cates; 2, A. H. Arnold; 3, D. W. Chapman; 4, W. A. James.
58. **Vase Three Specimen Blooms.** 1, B. W. W. Sampson; 2, G. R. Mack; 3, A. A. J. R. Millward; 4, C. E. Newman.

Restricted to Amateurs who have never won a first prize at any exhibition of the Society

59. **One Vase,** six stems. 1, W. J. Widgery; 2, N. A. Gibson; 3, F. E. Taylor.
60. **Box Six Specimen Blooms.** 1, C. Sales; 2, C. E. Sanson; 3, J. F. Newton; 4, B. J. Gibbs.
61. **Vase Six Specimen Blooms.** 1, Rev. T. Ewbank; 2, C. Sales; 3, Windsor Spice.
62. **Vase Three Specimen Blooms,** distinct. 1, J. F. Newton; 2. P. Knight; 3, C. Sales; 4, H. J. Roff.
63. **Vase Three Specimen Blooms.** 1, G. R. Mack; 2, H. Sumner; 3, L. W. G. Skinner; 4, J. F. Newton.

Restricted to Amatuers who have never previously exhibited at any exhibition of the Society

64. **One Vase,** Six stems, 1, A. W. Liquorish; 2, J. F. Newton; 3, Lady Wigram.
65. **One Vase,** Six stems, any varieties. 1, H. Sumner, 2, Dr. A. C. V. Gossett; 3, C. W. Spencer; 4, G. E. Revis.

Restricted to provincial members resident 100 miles or more from London

66. **The Franklin Dennison Memorial Bowl.** One vase, eight stems. 1, A. Cobley; 2, D. Pope; 3, E. H. Ackerman.
67. **Three Vases,** five stems in each. 1, D. Pope, 2, E. M. Allen; 3, W. H. Pilkington.
68. **Two Vases,** three blooms in each. 1, E. M. Allen 2, A. Cobley; 3, D. Pope.

AFFILIATED SOCIETIES

69. **The Franklin Dennison Memorial Cup.** One bowl H.T. Roses and one bowl Hyb. Poly. or Poly. Roses. 1, Harrow Horticultural Society; 2, Eastcote Horticultural Society; 3, Ibis Horticultural Society.

ARTISTIC CLASSES

70. **Dinner Table Decoration.** 1, Miss G. Woollard; 2, Mrs. L. A. Gotobed; 3, Miss E. Hambly Parker.
71. **Dinner Table Decoration** (grown in the open). 1, Mrs. D. Thorn; 2, Miss G. Woollard; 3, Miss A. M. Aldous; 4, Mrs. A. E. Barker.
72. **Sideboard Decoration.** 1, Miss A. M. Aldous; 2, Mrs. M. E. Barton; 3, Mrs. H. G. Clacy; 4, Miss E. Hambly Parker.

Restricted to Amateurs who grow and stage without assistance

73. **The Queen Alexandra Memorial Trophy.** Dinner Table Decoration. 1, Miss G. Woollard; 2, Mrs. H. G. Clacy; 3, Mrs. Barnes; 4, Mrs. G. E. Dalton.
74. **Bowl of Mixed Roses.** 1, Mrs. H. G. Clacy; 2, Mrs. P. Johnson; 3, Mrs. A. E. Griffith.

NOVICE CLASS

75. **Bowl of Mixed Roses.** 1, Mrs. M. Anstiss; 2, Mrs. M. Latimer; 3, Mrs. E. Toogood; 4, Miss E. Pickering.

THE PROVINCIAL ROSE SHOW, MANCHESTER

OLIVER MEE, O.B.E., Deputy President

MEMBERS of the N.R.S., in particular those in the North-Western Counties, anticipated July 25th and 26th with more than usual interest ; the occasion being the Provincial Rose Show in Platt Fields Park, Manchester, held in conjunction with the Annual Flower Show sponsored by the Manchester City Council. It may be of interest to recall that the first N.R.S. Provincial Show was held in Manchester in 1879, and the last time it was held in the district was in 1936, the venue on that occasion being Alderley Edge, a residential suburb situated some fourteen miles south of the City.

Well : The Show dates duly arrived and, as befitted the importance of the event, so did the President, Deputy President, a Past President ; six Vice-Presidents as well as reponsible officials of the Society. Also, there was a distinguished and very welcome visitor in Dr. Charles Covell, Past President of the American Rose Society, accompanied by his wife, who *en route* by air to the Continent had broken their flight in England to attend the Provincial Show. Dr. Covell paid high tribute to the excellence of the exhibits staged by both amateurs and nurserymen. After seeing the Show he, at his own suggestion, was taken to see gardens of Roses in Cheshire, including the Municipal Rose Garden, Stockport, in which there are 4,473 Rose trees in 29 varieties, including many of the latest introductions to commerce.

And what of the weather in Manchester during the Show(!) it certainly warrants comment. There was brilliant sunshine on both days, and with a temperature of 80 degrees upwards, exhibitors and visitors alike were virtually reduced to the proverbial " grease-spots." During the Show—and for many days prior—there was not one drop of rain ! Thus Manchester belied its reputation and gave the lie to the Music-Hall " gags " about the weather. Need I observe I claim to be a Manchester man ! As a point of interest it should be noted that the official record of the rainfall during 1951 was, London (over the Thames basin above Teddington) 39.56 inches ; Manchester 36.66 inches. But Manchester men, like Scotsmen and Scots jokes, enjoy and encourage this joke for, despite the drought and heat, several were to be seen during the Show with a mackintosh or carrying an umbrella.

But because of a period of drought and an exceptional season for Roses, the Show occurred during a " lean " period for Amateur Rosarians ; that is to say, between the first and second crop of blooms ; even so, the exhibits staged were remarkably good. The competitors included many of the well-known exhibitors at Shows in the Northern Counties, as well as notable amateurs from the South.

The Jubilee Trophy, awarded for the highest aggregate number of points in Divisions " A " and " B " for amateurs, was won by Mr. J. A. Gibson, Formby, Lancashire, and the N.R.S. Medal for the best Rose in the Amateur Classes was given for a fine specimen bloom of Ena Harkness shown by Mrs. M. Machin, Cheadle Hulme, Cheshire.

The new seedling Roses, as usual, attracted connoisseurs and the general public. Three Gold Medals were awarded and three Certificates of Merit to the following seedlings :—

Gold Medals

Bacchus (H.T.), bright scarlet, shown by Alex. Dickson and Sons, Ltd.

Siren (Floribunda), orange scarlet, shown by Wheatcroft Bros., Ltd.

Brilliant (H.T.), bright red, shown by Wheatcroft Bros., Ltd.

Certificates of Merit

Salmon Perfection (Floribunda), shown by Alex. Dickson and Sons, Ltd.

Poulsen's Supreme (Floribunda), shown by Samuel McGredy and Son.

Moulin Rouge (Floribunda), shown by Wheatcroft Bros., Ltd.

In the classes for the trade eight nurserymen staged attractive stands of Roses in wide variety and first rate quality. The best bloom in the Nurserymen's Section was adjudged to be Comtesse Vandal, shown in Class 1 by Alex. Dickson and Sons, Ltd.

The Jubilee Trophy and a Gold Medal for a representative group of cut Roses arranged for effect on a space 20-ft. by 4-ft., was won by Wheatcroft Bros., Ltd.

In the competitive classes for nurserymen Gold Medals were also awarded to J. Townsend and Sons ; Chas. Gregory and Sons, Ltd., and Fryers Nurseries, Ltd. Superb exhibits in non-competitive classes were staged by Alex. Dickson and Sons, Ltd., Sam McGredy and Son, and Dickson and Co. The Manchester Flower Show Committee awarded Gold Medals to the first two, and to the last a Silver Gilt Medal. And whilst, in general, the blooms of the numerous varieties staged were of excellent quality, those impressively shown, attracting special interest, included Charles Gregory (H.T.), Fashion (Floribunda), Gay Crusader (H.T.), Independence (H.T.), Show Girl (H.T.) and Masquerade (Floribunda).

Groups of Roses staged on Island Sites have become a popular feature. Too often they are strictly symmetrical and very formal in style ; in this connection the design applied by Chas. Gregory and Sons, Ltd., deserves mention. It was a pleasing and attractive breakaway from the traditional. The bowls and pillars of Roses were displayed to full advantage and though somewhat irregular in outline an overall general balance was maintained. The set-up was artistic and impressive, attracting much attention.

"*For paynes of the heed caused of heate, anoynte the foreheed and the temples. And do thus to the fayntnes that wykeneth the body and that cometh of weykenesse of the herte. But it is better to meddle the sayde oyle with powdre of seed sandalles or whyte or at leest powder of Roses. Also for the above sayd diseases, put oyle of Roses in the pacyentes meate in stede of comyn oyle and chiefly against chauffyng of ye liver.*

"*For the gommes that ben gnawen and frette with evyl humours. Sette clowse into Rose water and then drye them and make thereof powder.*"

Turners Herball, 1568.

THE AUTUMN ROSE SHOW

A. G. L. HELLYER

IT is no use pretending that the Autumn Show, held in the Royal Horticultural Society's New Hall on Friday, September 19th, was the best ever. There was too much evidence of weather damage for that. All the same it was a most interesting show and perhaps all the more instructive because the rather unkindly weather that preceded it did give us a chance to assess the weather resisting qualities of many new Roses. I thought Spek's Yellow came out with particular credit for it was the brightest and cleanest flower in many exhibits.

Taking the big groups first, R. Harkness and Co., again secured the Challenge Cup in Class I for an exhibit on a space 15 feet by 4 feet. This was an outstanding exhibit, well staged with nicely rounded masses of good, clean flowers. Lady Belper was particularly lovely and I was also glad to see Gordon Eddie in very good shape. It is an attractive warm peach Hybrid Tea with a flush of deeper colour that gives it warmth.

John Mattock was second and had a Gold Medal. He had some immensely showy blooms of Tally Ho, a carmine H.T. that seems destined to repeat its American success over here. I also noted a very nice deep yellow Rose named Lydia which I had not seen before. It is not unlike Spek's Yellow, which is high praise in itself.

The third prize and a Silver-gilt Medal went to Frank Cant and Co. They had Grandmaster showing really lovely colour. This I feel sure is going to be everybody's favourite for a good many years to come. Incidentally Ophelia was so lovely and so clean in this exhibit that I am sure it would have drawn a crowd had it been a novelty.

Both Chaplin Bros. and E. W. Stedman had Silver Medals. The first named could have done with more flowers, a criticism that applies even more to Mr. Stedman's group. Chaplins were showing United Nations very well and I found myself asking again what I have asked before, why is such an attractive Floribunda so little seen ? Mr. Stedman had good blooms of Masquerade, a Rose which

I began by heartily disliking but which undoubtedly improves on acquaintaince.

First place in Class 2 for a group on a space 10 feet by 4 feet, was secured by Stephen Treseder and Son. This was another exhibit in the Harkness style, well filled with good blooms, and it thoroughly deserved its award. Spek's Yellow was particularly fine here, some of the flowers being much larger than we are accustomed to expect from this very free flowering variety. I also stopped to admire the brilliance of Mary Wheatcroft. For colour I like it the best of the Mrs. Sam McGredy group.

Second place in this class was taken by Henry Drew who had plenty of good flowers but did not make the best of them, partly, I think, because his main pillars were too narrow. Glory of Rome was really magnificent in this exhibit, the deep rose flowers being huge and excellently formed.

Gandy Roses, Ltd., were third. Again there was a failure to make the most of the material available and the mechanics of staging showed far too much. I had not previously seen Daphne Gandy, a useful looking scarlet Floribunda, but the Rose that particularly pleased me here was Heidekind. It is a brilliant cherry-pink Floribunda and it has an unusually compact habit, but I find it a little subject to black-spot. Nevertheless I rate it high.

The outstanding entry in the class for an exhibit on an island site 12 feet by 8 feet, was undoubtedly that staged by C. Gregory and Sons. It had the De Escofet Memorial Cup and a Gold Medal, and I do not imagine that it took the judges long to make up their minds. This was a group on the grand scale in which large vases on pedestals were superimposed on a great, dome-like mass of bloom. Long branches of Rosa omeiensis pteracantha, which stood up like plumes above this exhibit, rather muddled the effect and were, perhaps, the only false touch. The flowers were as good as the arrangement and I made numerous notes including Flaming Sunset as a delightfully soft bi-colour ; Border King as a brilliant scarlet Floribunda with something a little different about its colouring ; and Pompon Beauty, looking less like a Rose and more like a double geranium than ever.

The exhibit of W. Lowe and Son, Ltd., who were second and were awarded a Silver-gilt Medal, was rather square built, an arrangement which resulted in many of the blooms being partially hidden.

Third place and a Silver-gilt Medal were awarded to Blaby Rose Gardens, the centre of whose group was staged in the form of a rather high cone. It made a most effective mass of colour. A notable maize-yellow Rose was Geheimrat Duisberg, but I cannot see it going far in England with a name like that.

Wheatcroft Bros., Ltd., arranged a big, non-competitive group in the centre of the hall, and brought a lot of their own introductions. I have never seen Pigalle in such good form. It is not a Rose I like, but as seen on that day I can well understand that some people would find great delight in its huge, cabbagy blooms with their curious mixture of petunia purple and yellow parchment. Cocorico I regard as one of the outstanding bedding Roses and Tzigane is probably the best bi-colour even if its autumn colour is a little harsh.

Some of the best blooms of Ena Harkness and of Spek's Yellow to be found in the show were in a rather disjointed group arranged by Dickson and Co., Edinburgh. Alex Dickson and Sons, Ltd., of Newtownards, made good use of Signora which is a long and lovely flower of brightest cherry flushed with yellow. They also showed Texas Centennial well enough to make one understand why it ranks so high in America.

E. B. Le Grice made a central pillar to his exhibit with several different Roses and surrounded this rather too sparsely with bowls. Dusky Maiden and Dainty Maid were two of his best varieties.

What a good bright Floribunda Tantau's Triumph is. It has a touch of the Independence colour about it and draws the eye at once. Ben. R. Cant and Sons had it in nice condition, but could have done with more blooms of all the varieties they staged.

G. F. Letts arranged their blooms in the form of a small Rose garden with beds to colour. It was nicely done and effective.

John Waterer, Son and Crisp made a particularly pleasant arrangement of bowls and baskets in which they included some of the most attractive Floribunda varieties such as Frensham, Poulsen's Pink (how delightfully the various shades of pink in this flower blend) and Anne Poulsen. Marcel Gret is a very fine yellow H.T.

Another imitation Rose garden with cut flowers arranged to look like growing bushes was made by Jordans English Rose Tree

Co. This was particularly well conceived and deserved a better place as it was rather hidden away in one of the aisles.

A small but attractive group from Messrs. Bakers contained that very showy bi-colour Gay Crusader and also an exceptional, richly coloured gold Rose with a hint of orange, named Doreen. I had not met this variety before but now I shall watch for it with interest.

Sam McGredy and Sons filled a large wall space with some most interesting flowers. Probably the best was Pink Spiral, which is well named as it is a real rose pink and the long, large flowers have a slightly spiralled shape. It is always risky to assess new Roses at a first meeting but I shall be surprised if this is not a winner.

An exhibit of great interest was that from A. Noordan, of Aalsmeer. It was marked " wholesale only " but it collected a crowd most of the time. Small wonder, for Poinsettia is a breath-taking scarlet, and Orange Delight a clear orange of a shade I know well enough in dahlias but had not met before in Roses. New Yorker, with shapely crimson flowers on long stems, and Tawny Gold, a good maize yellow, were others I found very pleasing here.

The class for 24 Roses in a box was won by Thanet Roses, who also had a Silver-gilt Medal for the best bloom shown by a nurseryman. This was a really lovely Ena Harkness. Other outstanding flowers here were Happiness, Spek's Yellow, McGredy's Triumph and Leading Lady.

A. C. Turner won the Challenge Cup offered in Class 4 for Roses shown in vases. Here again Ena Harkness and Spek's Yellow were outstandingly good and so was Mary Wheatcroft.

In the amateur classes M. L. Kemp had a really good day for he won the cup for 12 Roses in a Box in Division A,which is open to all amateurs, and repeated this success in Division B, which is restricted to amateurs who employ no labour. Congratulations, Mr. Kemp, on a well deserved success. Outstanding blooms in the Division A exhibit were Ena Harkness, Sam McGredy and John H. Ellis, and those I specially admired in his Division B dozen were George Dickson, May Wettern, Dr. F. G. Chandler and William Harvey.

I noticed with pleasure Mr. A. Norman's several wins in Division B, for he is an exhibitor who has ungrudgingly passed on his knowledge to thousands of other Rose growers, and it is good to see that the master can still hold his own. His box of six blooms was first class, and contained two blooms each of Dame Edith Helen, Ida McCracken and Ena Harkness. He also won with four vases of decorative Roses, and again used his own seedling, Ena Harkness, most effectively. Yet another success was with a bowl of decorative Roses.

Another very successful exhibitor in Division B was L. A. Anstiss who won Class 25 for six Roses in a box, and also had a first for two vases. The varieties in his box were J. H. Ellis, Candeur Lyonnaise, a very nice Show Girl, Peace and The Doctor.

Division C is restricted to amateurs who grow no more than 500 Roses and Division D to amateurs with no more than 250 Roses. As I always think the box classes provide the greatest test of cultural skill, I looked to see who was winning them in these two divisions and what manner of blooms they produced with such restricted supply. I was most impressed by what I saw, for C. F. Warren's six in the "500" Division would have taken a lot of beating anywhere, and C. H. Taylor's six in Division D were also very good. The first made use of Barbara Richards, William Harvey and two blooms each of Eden Rose and Peace. Mr. Taylor had Glory of Rome, John H. Ellis, Peace and William Moore.

The best bloom shown by an amateur was a lovely Glory of Rome shown by R. White, of Aylesbury.

In the decorative classes I particularly liked Mrs. C. A. Tisdall's lovely bowl in Class 11. She associated blooms of Lady Sylvia with the purplish grey foliage of one of the species, Rosa rubrifolia I think, but it was unnamed on the exhibit. Anyway the effect was delightful.

And so to the new Roses, only one of which secured a Gold Medal. This was Moulin Rouge, a Floribunda Rose that has now had so many awards that it must be regarded as the outstanding Rose of the year. At this show it also won the President's International Trophy and it has had an Award of Merit from the R.H.S. I like it for its well formed and firmly built flowers and for its vivid scarlet colour. Moulin Rouge was shown by Wheatcroft Bros.

There were four Certificates of Merit to Fred W. Alesworth, Irene of Denmark, Bonnie Maid and First Love.

Irene of Denmark may be the white Floribunda we have been looking for. It is odd that despite all the advance in coloured Roses good whites are still so scarce. Actually Irene of Denmark is not quite pure white for there is an occasional hint of pink. The flowers are borne in large clusters.

Bonnie Maid is another Floribunda. It starts by producing a shapely, spiralled bud and this opens to a big, semi-double flower not unlike Else Poulsen but a little deeper in colour. It is an attractive Rose which was well shown by E. B. Le Grice.

First Love is an H.T. of the Comtesse Vandal type. I doubt that it was seen to best advantage at this show and I shall watch for it next year with interest. It was shown by R. Harkness and Co.

PRIZE WINNERS—GREAT AUTUMN SHOW, 1952.

Class

NURSERYMEN

1. **Autumn Roses Challenge Cup.** A representative group, 15-ft. by 4-ft. 1, R. Harkness and Co.; 2, John Mattock; 3, F. Cant and Co.; 4, Chaplin Bros. and E. W. Stedman, Ltd.
2. **A Representative Group,** 10-ft. by 4-ft. 1, S. Treseder and Son; 2, H. Drew, 3, Gandy's Roses, Ltd.
3. **The De Escofet Memorial Cup.** Display of Roses, 12-ft. by 8-ft., on island site. 1, C. Gregory and Son, Ltd.; 2, Blaby Rose Gardens and W. Lowe and Son, Ltd.; 3, B. R. Cant and Sons, Ltd.; and E. B. Le Grice.
4. **The A. C. Turner Challenge Cup.** Distinct varieties. 1, R. M. Tooke; 2, R. C. Ferguson and Sons; 3, J. Townsend and Sons.
5. **Two Baskets Hybrid Polyantha Roses,** distinct. 1, J. Townsend and Sons; 2, S. Treseder and Son; 3, R. M. Tooke.
6. **Two Baskets Polyantha Roses,** distinct. 1, F. Cant and Co.
7. **One Basket,** one variety. 1, R. C. Ferguson and Son; 2, J. Townsend and Sons; 3, S. Treseder and Son.
8. **Twenty-four Specimen Blooms in Boxes.** 1, C. Longley (Roses), Ltd.; 2, F. Cant and Co.; 3, R. C. Ferguson and Sons.
9. **Twelve Blooms,** distinct. 1, Thomson and Henderson; 2, R. C. Ferguson and Sons; 3, J. Townsend and Sons.
10. **Dinner Table Decoration.** 1, Mrs. Tisdall; 2, Miss J. Wheatcroft; 3, H. Drew; 4, S. Eacott.
11. **Bowl of Roses.** 1, Mrs. Tisdall; 2, F. Carter; 3, E. B. Le Grice; 4, J. Townsend and Sons.

AMATEUR—Open Classes

13. **Bowl Roses,** 18 stems. 1, R. White; 2, J. R. Colyer; 3, L. P. Roberts.
14. **Bowl Hybrid Polyantha or Polyantha Roses,** 12 stems. 1, R. White; 2, J. R. Colyer, 3, E. M. Allen.
15. **Six Vases Roses,** distinct. 1, E. M. Allen; 2, W. H. Pilkington; 3, L. P. Roberts.
16. **The N.R.S. Challenge Cup.** Box 12 specimen blooms, distinct. 1, M. L. Kemp; 2, W. J. Northfield.
17. **Box Six Specimen Blooms.** 1, E. Royalton Kisch, 2, L. P. Roberts.
18. **Two Vases Specimen Blooms,** three in each. 1, R. White; 2, C. C. Williamson; 3, Mrs. M. Bulman.

Amateurs who grow and stage without assistance

19. **Bowl of Roses,** 18 stems. 1, A. Norman; 2, E. H. Ackerman; 3, W. J. Northfield.
20. **Bowl of Roses,** 12 stems. 1, E. H. Ackerman; 2, A. W. J. Green; 3, F. Fairbrother; 4, W. J. Northfield.
21. **Bowl Hybrid Polyantha or Polyantha Roses,** 12 stems. 1, D. Pope; 2, E. Royalton Kisch, 3, L. A. Anstiss.
22. **Four Vases,** distinct varieties. 1, A. Norman; 2, W. J. Northfield, 3, M. L. Kemp.
23. **The N.R.S. Challenge Cup.** Box 12 specimen blooms. 1, M. L. Kemp; 2, A. Norman; 3, C. F. Warren.
24. **Box Six Specimen Blooms,** three distinct. 1, A. Norman; 2, W. H. Beckett, 3, L. A. Anstiss.
25. **Box Six Specimen Blooms.** 1, L. A. Anstiss; 2, A. W. J. Green; 3, M. L. Kemp.
26. **Two Vases Blooms,** three in each. 1, L. A. Anstiss; 2, W. J. Northfield; 3, F. Fairbrother.
27. **Vase Four Specimen Blooms.** 1, J. E. Eld; 2, L. A. Anstiss; 3, A. W. J. Green; 4, A. Norman.

Restricted to growers of not more than 500 trees who grow and stage without assistance

28. **Bowl of Roses,** twelve stems. 1, W. C. Thorn; 2, E. E. Gatward, 3, J. E. Eld; 4, A. Cobley.
29. **Bowl of Hybrid Polyantha or Polyantha Roses,** nine stems. 1, C. Somerset; 2, Mrs. D. Walker; 3, T. Bridgstock.
30. **Four Vases,** distinct varieties. 1, T. Bridgstock, 2, H. C. Wilson; 3, Mrs. D. Walker.
31. **Box Six Specimen Blooms.** 1, C. F. Warren; 2, T. Bridgstock; 3, A. E. Barton; 4, W. C. Thorn.
32. **One Vase,** three blooms. 1, J. E. Eld; 2, W. E. Bish; 3, Miss B. Somerset; 4, A. E. Barton.
33. **Bowl Six Specimen Blooms.** 1, Mrs. A. C. Newman; 2, R, Bridgstock; 3, A. E. Barton; 4, J. E. Eld.

Restricted to growers of not more than 250 trees who grow and stage without assistance

34. **Three Vases,** distinct variety in each. 1, W. H. Beckett; 2, G. Walters; 3, C. H. Taylor.
35. **Bowl Hybrid Polyantha or Polyantha Roses,** six stems. 1, Mrs. M. H. Bristow; 2, Mrs. A. C. Newman; 3, E. H. Pollitt; 4, C. Somerset.
36. **Bowl Hybrid Polyantha or Polyantha Roses,** six stems, one variety. 1, Mrs. A. K. Wort; 2 C. Somerset; 3, C. H. Taylor.
37. **Box Six Specimen Blooms.** 1, C. H. Taylor; 2, Mrs. M. H. Bristow; 3, W. H. Beckett.
38. **Vase Three Specimen Blooms,** distinct varieties. 1, G. Walters; 2, Mrs. A. C. Newman; 3, D. W. Chapman; 4, Mrs. M. H. Bristow.
39. **Vase Three Specimen Blooms.** 1, J. E. Wiseman; 2, D. W. Chapman; 3, E. H. Pollitt; 4, G. Walters.

METROPOLITAN CLASSES

Restricted tc Amateurs living within a radius of 12 miles from London

40. **Bowl of Roses,** twelve stems. 1, D. L. Flexman; 2, Miss M. Gardener; 3, L. Hollis.
41. **Box Six Specimen Blooms.** 1, W. A. James; 2, Miss M. Gardener; 3, S. Phillips.
42. **Vase Six Specimen Blooms.** 1, Miss M. Gardener; 2, H. C. Wilson; 3, S. Phillips.

Restricted to Amateurs who have never won a first prize at any exhibition of the Society

43. **Vase Roses,** six stems. 1, C. W. A. Heyes; 2, A. W. Redford; 3, J. B. Edmans.
44. **Box Six Specimen Blooms.** 1, C. H. Clark; 2, C. W. A. Heyes; 3, B. J. Gibbs and N. A. Gibson.
45. **Vase Six Specimen Blooms.** 1, R. C. Balfour; 2, N. A. Gibson, 3, Mrs. F. E. Barker.
46. **Vase Six Specimen Blooms,** distinct varieties. 1, J. W. O. Lawrence, 2, E. H. Lockton; 3, J. B. Edmans; 4, C. H. Clark.
47. **Vase Three Specimen Blooms.** 1, A. W. Redford; 2, R. C. Balfour; 3, J. W. O. Lawrence; 4, C. H. Clark

Restricted to Amateurs who have never previously exhibited at any exhibition of the Society

48. **Vase Roses,** six stems. 1, C. H. Clark; 2, Mrs. E. Wilcox.
49. **Vase Roses,** six stems, any varieties. 1, J. W. O. Lawrence; 2, E. Wonnacott; 3. A. E. V. Walduck.

Restricted to provincial members resident 100 miles or more from London

50. **Bowl Roses,** six stems. 1, E. H. Ackerman; 2, E. M. Allen; 3, A. Cobley; 4, G. W. Chadwick.
51. **Three Vases,** four stems in each. 1, E. H. Ackerman; 2, E. M. Allen; 3, D. Pope.
52. **Two Vases Specimen Blooms,** three in each. 1, E. M. Allen; 2, A. Cobley; 3, E. H. Ackerman.

ARTISTIC CLASSES

53. **Dinner Table Decoration.** 1, Mrs. G. E. Dalton, 2, Mrs. F. E. Barker, 3, Mrs. P. Johnson.

Restricted to Amateurs who grow and stage without assistance

54. **Dinner Table Decoration.** 1, Mrs. D. Thorn; 2, Mrs. M. Latimer; 3, Mrs. P. Johnson.
55. **Bowl of Mixed Roses.** 1, Mrs. Temple Twining; 2, Mrs. M. E. Barton; 3, Mrs. P. Johnson.

NOVICE CLASS

56. **Bowl of Mixed Roses.** 1, Mrs. Blewett; 2, Mrs. E. Toogood; 3, Mrs. M. Latimer.

"NO FLOWERS, BY REQUEST"

In Memory of A. Norman Rogers

(President 1945-46; Honorary Treasurer, 1934-1948)

He loved roses; and his place of rest
Would have been heaped with too-soon-fading flowers
Reprieved to live all their allotted hours
Because he wished " No flowers, by request."
His roses loved him—gave him of their best,
Gracing his garden, winning honour due
To perfect growth and perfume, form and hue;
Therefore he wished " No flowers, by request."
And we all loved him—human, kindly, wise—
Welcomed his coming, hailed his patient smile;
Not one complaint, though racked with pain the while!
Should there be roses out beyond the skies
Perhaps this great Rose-lover may be found
Awarding points in Heaven's Trial-ground.

A. M. A.

THE BRISTOL SHOW

A. E. GRIFFITH, Past-President

THIS Bristol Group is doing an effective job, enlarging its field of activities and is meeting with such success that it is deserving of all the support that the parent body can give. Its fifth Show was held at The Corn Exchange, Bristol, on July 2nd, 1952, and was very well supported by both the Amateur growers and the Nurserymen who specialize in Roses.

It must be very gratifying to all concerned to get the splendid support from the trade, without which the Show would be a very different affair.

The luncheon was graced by the presence of the Lord Mayor and Lady Mayoress, Alderman and Mrs. V. J. Ross, and after an excellent lunch at the Grand Hotel all speeches were commendably brief, the chief guest after an excellent speech being followed by The President of The National Rose Society, Mr. D. L. Flexman, Mr. W. J. W. Sanday, Mr. Edgar Allen and the Hon. Secretary of The Bristol Group, Mr. E. R. Tizard. It was abundantly clear that Rose growing does not detract from a keen sense of humour and the short speeches, all too short, of Mr. Allen and Mr. Tizard set the table in a roar. This was a most enjoyable gathering and it is a safe thing to say that " a good time was had by all."

The Trade Groups made an excellent show, Messrs. Stephen Treseder and Son taking the Challenge Cup for the best display together with a Gold Medal Card award. Messrs. James Townsend and Sons also secured a Gold Medal Card award and Silver Gilt awards were made to Messrs. John Sanday (Roses) Ltd., and Messrs. H. Williamson and Company with Silver awards to Messrs. English and Sons and Messrs. Denys Lawrence. Top marks went to Messrs. John Sanday (Roses) Ltd. for the Nurserymen's 24 blooms.

The Artistic Classes were well supported, the bowl of Roses by Mrs. Sanday being a very noticeable arrangement and gaining the Perpetual Challenge Bowl of *The Western Daily Press and Bristol Observer*. Mention must be made of the many fine exhibits of Mr. Edgar Allen, of Bideford, who not only secured the Victor Osmond Challenge Bowl for the most points in the Amateur Classes, but also the Society's Bronze Medal for the best bloom by an Amateur

SOUVENIR JACQUES VERSCHUREN (H.T.)
Raised by J. Verschuren Pechtold, Holland.
Distributed by C. Gregory & Son, Ltd., Chilwell, Notts.
First Class Trial Ground Certificate, 1950.

exhibitor, a fine specimen of Sam McGredy. Mr. Bertram Park had firsts for a splendid bowl of De Ruiter's Herald and for a fine bowl of 18. Lt.-Col. D. Pope took firsts for a vase of Else Poulsen and for a bowl of 18 blooms. Mr. E. R. C. Tizard had several good entries, including a first for a vase of ramblers, whilst some very good exhibits were staged by Mr. W. H. J. Sansum. The Ladies' Artistic Classes were well filled, Table Decorations and Bowls of Roses adding greatly to the attractive appearance of the whole Show. Mrs. J. Hillier took a first for a well arranged table and Mrs. W. J. W. Sanday had four first prizes for some excellent displays.

Altogether this was a most successful Show upon which Mr. Sanday and all his efficient helpers are to be heartily congratulated.

"*Ah! what should we be without the Rose?*

Our poets sing of the rosy fingers of aurora, the rosy arms of the nymphs, the cheeks of Venus tinted with Roses.

The Rose is useful to the sick; she braves the duration of years; agreeable even in decay, she preserves the perfume of her youth.

What shall I say of her origin? When the sea formed from her froth, and displayed on her waves the beautiful Venus, brilliant with dew,—When Pallas sprang armed from the brain of Jupiter, the earth brought forth this admirable plant, a new masterpiece of nature. Eager to hasten her blooming, the gods watered her with nectar, and then this immortal flower elevated herself majestically on her thorny column. The Queen of Flowers."

Anacreon. Ode 51, The Rose.

SOUTHPORT SHOW, 1952

J. ROSCOE

EVEN with Southport's reputation, it is doubtful whether so fine a show has ever been staged in the large marquee as that seen on the 27th August, 1952.

The trade certainly reached a high standard in the production and staging of flowers and vegetables. It was rather surprising that the judges did not award a single gold medal to the trade Rose displays, for the groups were well up to standard especially those from north of the border, where the season is later. Messrs. Crolls, of Dundee, included some of the older Roses and Frau Karl Druschki was shown to perfection. Messrs. Wheatcroft's collection included several novelties, one of which was the almost black variety Tassin. There was nothing outstanding in new H.T. Roses, but the polyanthas Pompon Beauty and Border Queen shown by Gregorys, of Chilwell, were striking as was Masquerade on McGredy's Stand.

The amateur exhibits were an improvement on recent years, and it was a pity that these classes were pushed into a corner of the vegetable tent, instead of their usual place amongst the cut flowers.

Mr. F. A. Gibson, of Formby, was a prominent exhibitor and the two National Rose Society medals were won by Mrs. J. Roscoe and C. F. Warren. The special National Rose Society section was well supported, especially the vase classes. The boxes of specimen blooms, though not numerous, were well staged, and I still consider this type of exhibit to be the cream of the Rose classes at any show, for, as a Lancashire nurseryman once told me, it takes a good Rose grower to produce "good big 'uns !"

¶ The Hon. Editor is always glad to receive short articles from members. There must be many useful tips, home made gadgets or tools which they would like other members to know about. Manuscripts should be submitted by **mid-September**, and good photographs are particularly welcome.

FORMBY SHOW, 1952

J. ROSCOE

FOR Rosarians of Lancashire and Cheshire, Formby is always a happy rendezvous for the date of the event on the second Saturday of July usually coincides with the first flush of blooms in all their splendour. The standard of exhibits is exceptionally high and a first at Formby is certainly an achievement.

This year for the Rose classes there was a record entry, but the weather prior to the Show upset the calculations of some who had entered and cancellations were more numerous than usual. The Roses on view were, however, of a high standard, both from the point of view of size and colour.

The trade was well represented by Fryer's of Knutsford, Wheatcrofts of Nottingham, and Wrights of Formby, and the judges were right in awarding a gold medal to each of them.

In the open classes, Mr. G. V. Day of Wallasey again won the premier award for a box of 18 blooms. Other prominent exhibitors were Mr. F. A. Gibson of Formby, Mr. C. F. Warren of Bramhall, and Mr. J. Roscoe of Formby. The latter won the medal for the best bloom in the open classes with a specimen of George Dickson, so rarely exhibited nowadays.

In the local classes the medals were won by Mr. F. A. Gibson and Mrs. A. Entwistle.

The N.R.S. Classes were again well supported as will be seen from the following details :—

Box of six specimen blooms (seven entries)—1, C. F. Warren, Bramhall ; 2, H. S. Hodgkinson, Upton ; 3, G. V. Day, Wallasey.

Vase of three specimen blooms (eight entries)—1, F. A. Gibson, Formby ; 2, Miss E. Keeley, Birkdale ; 3, E. R. Allen, Hightown.

Three vases of decorative Roses (five entries)—1, W. H. Pilkington, St. Helens ; 2, William Bowker, Wirral ; 3, F. A. Gibson.

One vase of decorative Roses (8 entries)—1, H. S. Hodgkinson ; 2, F. A. Gibson ; 3, J. Roscoe.

Next year will mark the sixtieth anniversary of the Show and the committee are anxious to make the event a record one in all respects.

HUMUS

S. B. WATKINS

(From the "Queensland Co-operator," by courtesy of the Editor of The Australian and New Zealand Rose Annual)

THIS particular ingredient of the soil is of the first importance in making soils fertile and in producing conditions for active growth. On the physical side of soil condition, it keeps the soil open, spongy and porous, so that water can pass through easily and air penetrate readily ; on the chemical side it is of value in that it promotes active bacterial growth and the soil bacteria are able to attack other organic matter added to the soil. In decomposing this added material, as well as the humus already present, the bacteria set free valuable chemical plant foods. Moreover, the organic matter acts like a selective sponge holding in its meshes available plant foods which in its absence would quickly be washed from the soil. Its presence is of economic importance, for by it chemical fertilizers added to the soil in small quantities from time to time in accordance with good gardening are retained for the benefit of plant growth. It can be maintained in the soil by regular applications of good farmyard or other organic manures.

A great deal of argument centres around organic versus inorganic or chemical fertilizing practice. One school condemns inorganic fertilizers even to the extent of claiming the plants' products produced under chemical fertilization are deficient in health-promoting principles. They claim that it is only when plants are grown with the aid of organic manures that the products are of any value as foods. This appears to be without true scientific foundation, as chemical analysis of foods produced by both kinds of practice reveal little if any differences, either in mineral salts, vitamins, or the more pronounced food essentials such as carbohydrates, proteins or fats.

In economic garden practice, using chemical fertilizers, the rule is little and often. Thus, the plants are able to take up a greater proportion of the added foods applied at frequent intervals as limited dressings or watered on in the form of solutions called liquid fertilizers or liquid manures. That chemical fertilizers alone are capable of supporting plant life and producing useful food crops is well demonstrated in the modern practice of hydroponics, now called soilless gardening. In these methods, the plants are grown in nutrient solutions which are circulated through a medium such as straw, sand, charcoal or ashes, in which the roots of the plants are set. No organic manures are utilised. In fact it is because they are unprocurable and soil is scarce that this method has been used by the Americans on certain Pacific islands.

All organic manures, no matter what their origin, have to pass through a process of decomposition in the soil or in heaps before their goodness is available to plant life. By this means the complex constituents (such as partially digested food matter, fibre, etc.) are broken down through the agencies of bacteria into a simple material called humus which holds the simple chemical plant foods produced from complex ingredients by bacterial activity. This spongy product added to the soil contains all the essentials for promoting healthy plant growth. If there is a shortage of such organic material, the gardener must supplement with chemical fertilizers. However, in order that the plants may receive as great a benefit as possible from the additions of chemical foods, the soil should carry as much humus as possible to absorb the added chemicals for the continued benefit of the plants. Thus, the town gardener who is unable to procure his full requirements of manure, should maintain the organic matter or humus in his soil at as high a level as possible, in order that he may secure the greatest benefits from added chemical fertilizers that he must of necessity use.

First, there must be a receptacle for holding the refuse. A pit dug in the ground in an out of sight corner will do. It can be of convenient size, say, six feet long, four feet wide, and three feet deep. Into one end of this a one foot layer of grass cuttings, straw, leaves, household refuse, and weeds can be thrown. The layer is dressed with a handful of superphosphate and sulphate of ammonia and covered with a three inch layer of soil. Then a second layer is added with similar additions of fertilizer and soil, and so on until the heap stands well above the surroundings. It will soon settle down into the hole. The contents should be kept moist but not saturated. After about six weeks the heap is turned over to the other end of the hole, and a new heap prepared in the vacated spot. The turned heap in another six weeks will be ready for spreading over the beds and digging in. Its place is taken by the second heap as it is turned for the first time. In this way, the compost heap can be kept in continuous production for the benefit of the garden.

"MY MASTERPIECE"

STORIES which lie behind the production of some world-famous Roses. A series of articles (which will be continued) by leading hybridists.

FRANCIS MEILLAND, Antibes, France.

On looking through one of our note-books whose pages were already yellowing, we came across, under the date 15th June, 1935, the traces of what might be described as " the first pollen-charged brush-stroke " which gave rise to Peace (Mme. A. Meilland), the Rose we consider to be one of the very best we have ever produced. It was inscribed under the number 3-35-40 which means that the combination which produced it was the third we made in 1935, and that it was the fortieth of the 50 subjects which had received favourable notice before we budded a few eyes from the small original plants.

M. FRANCIS MEILLAND AND M. A. MEILLAND

The data in our note-book tell us also that 55 flowers were fecundated under precisely similar conditions, and that, from these, 52 hips were obtained, whose seeds during the following year produced 800 little plants. The female Rose in Peace (Mme. A. Meilland), was Johanna Hill, the male Rose was an unknown seedling inscribed under the number 103-32-A, and came from Chas. P. Kilham fecundated by Margaret McGredy. What was our object in making this crossing ? The principal idea behind the 103-32-A crossing is still very clear in our mind, in spite of the interval of 20 years. At that time we were looking for a way of producing a resistant foliage and winter hardiness in copper coloured Roses, and that was why we chose Margaret McGredy which we much admired for its qualities as a strong hardy plant. Chas. P. Kilham, on the other hand, was an excellent female which we knew to be capable of transmitting its own characteristic shape and colour to its progeny.

From this cross between Chas. P. Kilham and Margaret McGredy sprang a vigorous Rose with a bi-coloured flower and extremely brilliant colour, whose shape, however, left something to be desired. Its flowers also were most capricious, sometimes quite magnificent, at others frankly ugly. At one moment indeed, we seriously considered the idea of disseminating this variety which we had been subjecting to a most rigorous selection, but we finally abandoned this idea as we judged that our original object had not been attained. Since then, but not before we had used it successfully as the male progenitor of the Rose Peace (Mme. A. Meilland), we have lost this variety ; we regret this at times because it would have been useful to us in the pursuit of certain problems. The object we had in view with the Johanna Hill × (Chas. P. Kilham × Margaret McGredy) cross was to produce a new Rose of great hardiness, with very long shoots and with a robust and decorative foliage similar to that of Margaret McGredy. As for its colour, this would no doubt vary between yellow and a bi-coloured red and yellow, in other words it would have a pretty wide range.

Experience having proved that the characteristics conditioning the shape of Ophelia's flowers were dominant, and reproduced themselves in its progeny as, for example, in Johanna Hill, we decided that this Rose was the best variety to use, because of its fairly pronounced yellow colour. This Rose possessed the added advantage of developing a quite exceptionally erected vegetation, of being extremely hardy, and of producing buds, in every way, as well-shaped as those of Ophelia.

Such were the conditions governing the choice of begetters of the future Rose Peace (Mme. A. Meilland).

We still have a very clear picture in our minds of the exact place in the seedling frame occupied by the original plant of Peace (Mme. A. Meilland) among so many others whose colours varied from yellow and pale pink to more brilliant copper and some bi-coloured flowers, but these last rather rare.

It was not very sturdy, this little 3-35 plant, and there was nothing about it to attract attention. It was during the Summer of 1936 that a few eyes were budded for the first time. Budding certainly took place very early in the season because about October 10th, as my father and I were walking past the budded plants, we noticed their glossy foliage surmounted by large buds just about to open. Under the influence of extremely favourable weather conditions during that Autumn of 1936, these few buds produced flowers quite marvellous in shape and size with a greenish tinge, warming to yellow, and progressively impregnated with carmine round the edges of the petals. Systematic study of the 50 subjects obtained from the 800 seedlings showed nothing of great interest, with the single exception of the one marked 3-35-41 which was astonishingly like the one marked 3-35-40 with difference that, on opening, the flower was flatter, its colour less intense, and its foliage less resistant with a predisposition to chlorosis ; its stems moreover were much more thorny. Some years later plant number 3-35-41 was definitely set aside in favour of its sister 3-35-40 which was the only plant chosen from this cross.

In June, 1939, this plant proved the great revelation of the season and attracted the most attention among visitors. During that summer buds were sent to Germany, Italy and the United States. As we had no distributor in England at that time, buds might not be sent to that country until the following year.

With brutal suddenness, war broke out on the 3rd September, 1939, and all communication with Germany ceased. After the invasion of June, 1940, the same thing happened with Italy and then with England. The result was that the German firm which was to have distributed this Rose 3-35-40 put it on sale under the name Gloria Dei, and the Italian firm sold it under the name Gioia. In

France, my father and I decided to dedicate this Rose to the memory of my mother, Mme. A. Meilland, who had died a few years previously.

Before being admired by Rose lovers under its proper name 3-35-40 was particularly admired in Antibes where we were engaged in its propagation. The Comte de Martel, French High Commissioner in Syria at that time, was our neighbour. Accompanied by the Comtesse de Martel, the Duke of Windsor expressed a desire to visit our glasshouses and open air plantations, and spent over an hour doing so. He was most enchanted by 3-35-40 and said, to use his own words :—

> " I have never seen another Rose like it. It is certainly the most beautiful Rose in the whole world."

Until June, 1945, we had not the least idea as to what had become of this Rose in the United States. It was only then that the Conard Pyle Company told us of the successful experiments it had been making in cultivating it, and that, in agreement with certain other Rose growers of repute, it had been decided to call it Peace, to symbolise, as it were, the happy event which was to mark the end of the trials and suffering which the world had been experiencing for five years. The ceremony at which Peace was baptised took place under the auspices of the American Rose Society, after several months' notice of the event had been given. The date had been fixed for 29th April, 1945, which. by an extraordinary coincidence, was also that of the fall of Berlin.

Shortly after this a meeting of 49 delegations of the United Nations took place in San Francisco, and the heads of 49 delegations received, each in his own apartment a small vase with a single Rose Peace accompanied by the following message :—

> " *This is the Peace Rose which was christened at the Pacific Rose Society exhibition in Pasadena on the day Berlin fell. We hope the Peace Rose will influence men's thoughts for everlasting world peace.*"

We shall never forget all the emotions we have experienced by the creation of this Rose. The enthusiasm with which it has been received everywhere allows us to speak of it with the conviction that it is really the best Rose we have produced.

If circumstances have decided that it should be known by different names in different countries, this at least is true that each of these names reminds men of good will that the love of flowers, and in particular the admiration of this Rose will for ever provide them with the occasion to praise God, with Gloria Dei, to face life with a smile, with Gioia to wish for peace, with Peace and, as far as we ourselves are concerned, to perpetuate a loving memory, with Mme. A. Meilland.

A. NORMAN, Normandy, Surrey.

In stating which Rose one has raised should be termed one's " Masterpiece " is not quite so easy as it would seem, especially if one has the good fortune to raise several Roses of merit. The financial reward it has received is not always a sure guide to the answer, as popular taste is not necessarily the same as that of the raiser. However, assuming that for the purpose of this article the

A. NORMAN

term masterpiece means a Rose as near perfection as possible, I think floribunda Frensham would be my choice.

Although the cross made to produce this Rose was quite deliberate and with an idea of the outcome the seed parent was purely an accident of nature.

Having at the time a bed of mixed Orleans sports including Edith Cavell, I gathered some ripe seed that was on a plant of the latter overshadowed by a weeping standard of that old wichuraiana Edgar Andreu, a red variety not often seen in this country. In the seedlings raised from this seed was a rather pretty red polyantha quite unlike any of the others which were mostly pink and of little value. This red seedling showed its affinity to Edgar Andreu by its glossy foliage and general characteristics. As it set seed freely with its own pollen it was crossed with Crimson Glory, that Rose having just been put into commerce.

From this cross a Rose I called Haslemere was raised, which but for one fault (balled centre petals) might have become popular. From the next batch of seedlings came Frensham, but it was not until I had grown this for a couple of years that its good qualities were apparent. As a breeder it is quite sterile. I had hopes of another one from the same batch of seedlings, but that only got as far as ripening its pods without forming any seed in them. The extraordinary vigour of Frensham did not come directly from its seed parent, which was very dwarf and thin in growth, but from both the wichuraiana and multiflora strains. The rather abundant prickles were from its pollen parent Crimson Glory, and is probably its only fault. I have heard some mention of its liability to mildew and here again its wichuraiana parentage asserts itself, for one knows only too well how subject this class is to mildew when grown in a position which is unsuitable, and I have found on enquiry that where mildew has been troublesome, that it has been grown near a building, with the consequent draughts.

Many will wonder, I am afraid, why I have chosen Frensham instead of Ena Harkness, and I can only answer that it is quite possible that an improvement on the latter may be raised, difficult as that may be ! The chances of raising a seedling with all the necessary qualities that are essential, such as good growth (but not too good otherwise the interval between the flowering will be prolonged), freedom from disease ; good colour that does not fade to an unpleasing shade, fragrance, blooms held fairly erect, an adequate number of petals without tendency to divided centres, and ability to tolerate wet weather, is a remote possibility. Practically any one of these qualities being absent can make a Rose undesirable, and it is this fact that spurs on the raisers of new varieties, for although we have at the present time finer varieties than we have ever had before, very few have all these desirable qualities combined.

Lastly I would like to pay tribute to Wilhelm Kordes for giving to the Rose world that wonderful Rose Crimson Glory, for without that there would have been no Frensham or Ena Harkness, Red Ensign and William Harvey, to say nothing of the very many varieties that have been raised by other hybridists from this great Rose.

WILHELM KORDES, Holstein, Germany.

My dear Mr. Editor, you are asking for something I cannot give. None of my Roses is a "Masterpiece." Orange Triumph, Crimson Glory, Geheimrat Duisberg and a good many others all have their faults. They may sometimes bring all the wonder and all the beauty and perfume a Rose may be able to give and the next time be just as disappointing. So it is with Pinocchio, Independence (Kordes Soldermeldung) and Gertrude Westphal. But perhaps I will tell you a little Rose story instead.

The great man of Rosedom of my younger days, Monsieur Pernet-Ducher, sent out in 1908, Chateau de Clos Vougeot, a marvel when it has enough sunshine to bring out the deep crimson with black velvet of its large double flowers. Since then many breeders have tried to improve on the plant and give us that " black " Rose on a strong plant. Even Pernet sent out some H.T.s supposed to be improvements. Max Krause had the first real success in his Kardinal. From that I bred Crimson King and Mary Clay, but long before that Mallerin gave us Ami Quinard. The pollen from this gave me a near black but badly burning seedling with Robin Hood (Pemberton's) as seed parent. The pollen from this again on to long forgotten Aroma gave me Baby Chateau, and here the story begins. Baby Chateau is sometimes a beauty, but most times unsatisfactory, but as it is with mankind, a good soul may rest in the heart of even a loser in a beauty contest—so it is with this Rose. It gave to the Rose world the fiery cinnabar and scarlet hues that are more and more coming into our gardens and are being so hotly discussed. Direct seedlings of it are Tantau's Triumph, Independence (Kordes Sondermeldung), Florence Mary Morse and Gertrude Westphal. The second generation has given us Improved Tantau's Triumph,

WILHELM KORDES

Tantau's Delight, Bonn and so far an endless row of fiery coloured Roses in all shades of salmon and cinnabar and scarlet. The latest are seedlings that have the perfume we so much want in Roses and experience has shown us that the descendants of this one " lame duck," Baby Chateau, have that one great advantage over the older strains, they have *disease proof foliage*.

That is the story, you see that great Roseman, Pernet Ducher, gave me some imperfect Roses and I just married them. The result again fifty-fifty and at the end a rush of new colours and healthy plants.

So perhaps Baby Chateau is my real " Masterpiece."

E. B. Le GRICE, North Walsham, Norfolk.

E. B. LE GRICE

Before I come to the variety which I consider " My Masterpiece " I would like to say that every hybridist, as far as I see it, considers that his " Masterpiece " lies hidden in the future rather than revealed in the present. If he considers otherwise, I am sure that he would cease to cross with the high hopes that are his. " The best is yet to be," is surely his watchword.

Good hybridising should be the culmination of years of experiment, research and observation. The building up of a good strain rather than the individual variety should be the aim. To amplify this statement a little : It is possible to raise one outstanding variety by chance, but it is unlikely that other good sorts will be bred again from haphazard selection of parents. The real hybridist is seeking to build up a good strain where the outstanding novelty is the natural result of progressive improvement. A good strain from my point of view then should be not only good in itself but be capable of producing good progeny on either side. This is only possible where the strains have been proved and tested generation by generation. Nor does it follow that " My Masterpiece " might be considered the best of my seedlings by others. Outward looks alone cannot be the sole criterion.

With these preliminary remarks I would unhesitatingly place Dusky Maiden as my best yet. It is a hybridist's dream. The best qualities of parents and grandparents brought together in one seedling. It must be remembered that for one Dusky Maiden many other seedlings from the same cross, some with very good qualities, resulted and one in particular was grown beside her sister during the war years in open competition for pride of place. In the year 1931 when Daily Mail Scented was a very new Rose, I used it as pollen parent to Etoile de Hollande. I saw in my mind's eye a full petalled, sweetly scented vigorous Rose and of good shape. My records tell me that I crossed the varieties Etoile de Hollande and Daily Mail Scented both ways. It was the latter as seed parent that the single deep red seedling Rose came. It was my custom at the time to destroy all single flowered seedlings of Hybrid Teas as soon as they bloomed unless there was some outstanding quality of colour or similar desirable factor.

This seedling was saved for three reasons, the regularity of its five petals, the depth of colour and its sweet scent. It was budded and produced a medium grower with deep olive green foliage and a stem producing three flowers with regular insistance (it was an H.T. seedling). Two plants survived and were potted up. The first year I realised that possibilities lay in crossing Else Poulsen and this seedling. Pots of Else Poulsen were prepared and brought in the following spring. Else Poulsen's parentage (Orleans Rose × Red Star) and its frequent sports of a reddish type showed it would easily break from its pink colour, which must be recessive rather than dominant.

This proved to be the case and a number of red Hybrid Polyantha seedlings appeared. Many of these were excellent varieties, some lighter and a few darker than the parent. Growing on budded plants was now necessary if a fair test was to be made. A first sorting was immediately possible. Some were sprawling in character and showed other major faults. After three years two varieties were left. One to be finally known as Dusky Maiden, and the other, more free flowering and with larger trusses, but with brown anthers. Two qualities made the final decision in favour of Dusky Maiden, its golden anthers and its sweet perfume.

An analysis of the factors which came together in Dusky Maiden may be justified at this point. There were certain bad qualities present in some of the parents and grandparents, Daily Mail Scented had the great failing of burning badly. Its petals browned and crumpled with hot sun. Dusky Maiden retained the blackish maroon but does not burn in heat although a proportion of seedlings raised from it perpetuated this failing. From Daily Mail Scented it also obtained its very early flowering qualities, with us it is always the first Hybrid Polyantha to bloom. Else Poulsen has at least three bad failings, tendency to mildew, spotting of its flowers in the wet and the retention of its old blooms on the stems in unsightly masses, but it is a grand variety for freedom and continuity of flower. Dusky Maiden remains unaffected by wet, is very resistant to mildew, is very continuous and free and has a long flowering period, usually from late May to Christmas. It also sheds its petals leaving room for the young flowers to develop.

One might digress a moment to point out the importance of removing the old flower heads from such varieties as Dusky Maiden as seed pods develop rapidly and a plant cannot continue in flower and produce seed pods at the same time.

Last but not least its grandparent Etoile de Hollande gave the brilliant scarlet undertone to its blackish red and the scent is essentially also therefrom. It has been my experience that the "Etoile" type perfume and the elongated pedicel (the long flower stalk) are in the same chromosome and cannot be parted. If one is to be hypercritical then Dusky Maiden has this one failing, namely its individual flower stems are rather too long, but the other gift received from "Etoile," with its damask perfume, was its deep green abundant healthy foliage. Surely some fairy godmother was there to present so many gifts to one Rose and to pronounce so strong a spell as to exorcise so many potential failings at its birth. Perhaps the reader will appreciate with more understanding why this Gold Medal Rose claims first place in its raiser's affections and why he justifies it as his "Masterpiece."

MA PERKINS (hyb. poly.)
Raised by E. S. Boerner, Jackson and Perkins Co., New York
Distributed by Sam McGredy & Son, Portadown, and Alex Dickson & Sons, Belfast.

(For full description see page 150)

M. JEAN GAUJARD, Feyzin, France.

When we took over from Pernet-Ducher in 1924, we continued the line hybridising of his seedlings, and thus rapidly arrived at some Roses of perfect form, to attain, in 1934, to the variety Mme. Joseph Perraud. This novelty originated from a Pernet-Ducher seedling coming from Capucine Bicolore (R. foetida bicolor) as pollen parent with an unnamed seedling coming from Souv. de Claudius Pernet. This variety showed itself to have exceptionally good form with a colour which was at that time entirely new.

The remarkable origin of the Rose Mme. Joseph Perraud has made it an exceptional variety for hybridising. Most of the Rose hybridists of the world have worked on it and we ourselves have used it a great deal for many years. We have worked equally with other seedlings of Pernet-Ducher coming from Capucine Bicolore which have given us some varieties of a bright sparkling orange red, which we keep for further hybridising. It is these which we call our " stud." We used our " stud " to fertilise some descendants of Mme. Joseph Perraud and obtained in 1944 a quantity of seedlings of the orange red colouring. From amongst these we selected three Roses which have nearly related parentage—Opera, Ville de Gand and Madrigal. Madrigal had as seed parent, a seedling of Mme. Joseph Perraud × an unnamed. The seed parent of Ville de Gand was a seedling of Georges Chesnel × an unnamed, and Opera had the same seed parent as the last. Each of the seed parents of these three varieties were fertilised by seedlings of Mme. Joseph Perraud × Capucine Bicolore.

The three varieties have all been a great success but up to now Opera is perhaps considered " My Masterpiece." The colour, form and size of flower and the beauty of the foliage have made it a variety which has pleased the public, and for the last four years since it has become known, the number of plants grown has increased each year. It is, we consider, by its colouring and its foliage a notable step in the history of the Rose.

A number of Gold Medals have been gained by this variety and among others the Gold Medal of the National Rose Society in London in 1949.

For many years our method of work has always been the same. We work for " The Best." Maximum resistance to disease and the

JEAN GAUJARD

finest colour, on varieties which we call "commercial," that is to say *completely* satisfying in order to please the public. On the other hand we have a certain number of other varieties which have characteristics of great value which we do not issue, because they are not *completely* satisfying, they may be lacking in fullness of flower for instance or size, but we keep them for hybridising because they may have exceptional colour or they make a good plant, or germinate better than the average. We carefully keep those which may serve to improve existing varieties, amongst others we keep all those of a sparkling colour which show a good resistance to disease. We have observed that breeding from bad colour never gives plants of good colour. Deficiency of colour is hereditary.

We work also with varieties of other hybridists, especially those which have marked character either of colour or growth and foliage and if we obtain an interesting variety in the first generation, we cross it again with our " stud " to make an improvement, either in colour or size of flower, and so to obtain improved varieties for the public. It is thus that we have worked on Mme. Joseph Perraud and Georges Chesnel to arrive at Opera.

We have at the present time some types which are absolutely new as regards colour and foliage, with which we hope to continue the improvement of our varieties, and we hope to obtain more and more beautiful Roses.

HERBERT C. SWIM, Armstrong Nurseries, California, U.S.A.

My masterpiece as a Rose hybridizer is not yet produced. It is still in a stage of planning. If I were to admit that a Rose already on the market was my ideal or the best that I hope ever to be able to produce, I should be admitting to lack of imagination, a lack of confidence or a shortage of time. As yet, I am not convinced that any of these conditions apply.

My favorite among all of the Roses for which I am responsible is not one which has received any of the top international awards. It did receive a Certificate of Bagatelle and the First-Class Trial Ground Certificate from the National Rose Society. Even so, this Rose, which has been named First Love, is indeed first in my affection in the field of Rose varieties.

There are several reasons why this is so. In my garden, while it reaches definite peaks of flower, First Love is rarely ever out of bloom. The slender, graceful buds last exceptionally well when cut from the garden, although they are somewhat too small to be classified as exhibition type. It closely approaches my ideal as to gracefulness of the bud and the proportions existing between the size and length of the stem and the size of the bloom. While not immune to mildew, the foliage exhibits a high degree of resistance to the disease.

H. C. SWIM, Director of Research at Armstrong Nurseries

The foliage would be more attractive if it were larger and of a deeper color, but it is certainly not so lacking in these respects as to be conspicuous. The slenderness of the wiry, erect stems is a trait that fits into the general ensemble as indicated above. As it grows here I could wish that First Love have a few more petals with flowers of a somewhat larger size and more intense fragrance, yet, since experience teaches us that man is probably not capable of assisting in the creation of anything perfect even in his own eyes, First Love is very apt to be my favorite among my own varieties for a long time.

It is interesting to observe that First Love was produced as a result of crossing the two varieties introduced by the Armstrong Nurseries to win Gold Medals from the National Rose Society.

Charlotte Armstrong was the seed parent and Show Girl was the pollen parent of First Love. The cross came as close to producing the ideal contemplated in the planning stage as one can probably hope to achieve. It offers in combination many of the better qualities of the two parent varieties and to some extent omits their faults. What could be a more desirable result from the point of view of a Rose breeder ?

Some day I hope it may be my good fortune to produce a Rose with the vigor and productiveness, the gracefulness, daintiness, and consistency of First Love with such desirable qualities as complete immunity to at least the more important diseases, and with a more attractive foliage and a more intense fragrance than exists in this variety. If such a miracle were to come to pass I would still want to continue to breed Roses since I would then be inspired to reproduce this initial masterpiece in all of the colors to be found in the Rose family.

I have been asked to make a statement concerning my general policy as a hybridist. To some extent the objectives in the planning are disclosed above. In order to place the various characters in their proper relationship to one another, it perhaps should be stated that it seems that the primary objective of all Rose breeders should be to extend the range of Rose growing as it exists in the present so that many more people may obtain more enjoyment from Roses in the future. In analyzing the factors which relate to such basic objectives, it has seemed to me that such qualities as vigor, disease resistance, floriferousness, gracefulness and balance in the form of the buds and flowers, attractive foliage and pleasing fragrance of the flowers as well as their long lasting quality are all features that, if achieved, should contribute to these primary objectives in somewhat the order of importance in which I have mentioned them. There are, of course, many other qualities which might also contribute to this end, such as novelty of color, thornlessness, cold hardiness, and longevity.

Since such a campaign is obviously a very long term one, I may hope to achieve but few of these objectives, if indeed I may be permitted to achieve any of them. In the meantime, First Love will need to remain as my favorite and my masterpiece.

THE FUTURE OF THE ROSE

N. P. HARVEY

HILAIRE BELLOC and G. K. Chesterton considered that contemporary economic problems could be solved if " big business " were discouraged and industry reorganised as small units. Whether or not this would solve our troubles, is beside the point. Belloc and Chesterton were trying to put the clock back which is always impossiblle. The solution is undoubtedly to adapt present-day tendencies to our particular needs. To take a further parallel, we cannot expect the modern composer to write in the style of Bach and Handel.

The foregoing remarks are necessary for an understanding of the idea behind this article. Some enthusiasts seem anxious to hark back to the old-fashioned Roses, whether species or first and second crosses. Their attitude, though understandable, is mistaken. Many of the old-timers are still worth growing and are undeniably of great beauty, but Rose varieties of the future cannot be developed along the same lines, if only for strictly utilitarian reasons.

As long as Roses are propagated vegetatively on a large scale, deterioration of the individual variety will ultimately set in, and the regular production of new seedlings is therefore essential. They cannot be bred from worn-out varieties. Nor are the flat, cup shaped blooms and singles generally popular to-day.

Britain is still the stronghold of the individualist no matter what his political affiliations. Accordingly, the hybrid teas, though to some extent displaced by the newer floribundas, are still very widely grown (in the U.S.A. the gulf between the two groups is much wider). I believe the H.T.s will retain their popularity for many years and that certain developments as regards vigour, colour, fragrance and so on are both desirable and to a large extent possible, in the not too distant future.

Increased vigour is characteristic of nearly all post-war introductions. The shy-flowering purely exhibition H.T. is a rarity nowadays and a slightly smaller bloom will, I think, be always preferred to an immense, occasional flower. I must emphasise the word slightly, because contemporary exhibition type blooms like Red Ensign and Dorothy Anderson are only just behind Dame Edith Helen and Mrs. Charles Lamplough.

Disease incidence is still a difficult problem, and here progress is bound to be somewhat slow. Certain varieties, notably Peace, Independence and Karl Herbst, are highly resistant to black spot and mildew. Nevertheless, under very favourable conditions for mildew infection, I find that if spraying with a thiram or sulphur preparation is omitted, few, if any, varieties normally termed resistant, escape entirely, especially when growing near markedly susceptible kinds. I have seen mildew on all three varieties, admittedly to a limited extent. Most raisers discard any seedling showing a strong liability to disease, no matter how outstanding it may be in other directions. Unfortunately, there is another angle to the problem, as a variety which seems resistant may succumb years afterwards when it encounters a different strain of the same fungus.

To introduce one new characteristic into the hybrid tea group without losing those qualities it is essential to retain, may take a very long time. Would you want a variety virtually immune from disease but of mediocre colouring and poor shape ? Disease resistance often comes by accident rather than design. Most highly resistant varieties (at the moment there are comparatively few) have other virtues as well, but if we take Elmshorn, a newcomer in the hybrid musk group, one must admit that as far as colour goes, this Rose is undistinguished.

The answer as far as H.T.s are concerned, may entail the gradual breeding in of different foliage. I feel that this would in any case add to the aesthetic appeal of individual varieties. The greyish foliage of Rosa alba and its varieties such as Celestial and Maiden's Blush, is, I think, unsuited to the brilliant aggressive colours found in contemporary hybrid teas, but the shade of green found in the leaves of Rosa Moyesii might be welcome. The distinct shiny foliage of Mermaid and the reddish-grey foliage of R. rubrifolia are further examples.

If we consider colour, there is still plenty of scope. We shall, I think, secure brighter reds, especially in the scarlets. A pillar box red hybrid tea would be a real acquisition. Independence is a step forward, but though this variety holds its colour well in sunny weather, the blooms are often very dull during cool periods.

As regards dark reds, the position is still unsatisfactory. Crimson Glory remains the best, despite its faults. I cannot see much future for Charles Mallerin, the habit being ungainly and the plant not free enough.

A wider range of bicolours, often with less violent colour contrasts, seems possible, but they must have sufficient petals, be of good form and show reasonable colour stability in hot weather. Colour stability is very important on light, dry land. Very few bicolours and multi-colours are really satisfactory in this respect. Lack of sufficient petals is, however, less evident than in pre-war days.

Gay Crusader and Tzigane approximate to my ideal, but Sultane is too thin and fades rather quickly in strong sunlight. The same applies to Mme. Dieudonné. The flat cupped bicolours as represented by the old Condesa de Sástago are probably on the way out.

The American First Love, basically pink but showing different tones of the same colour, is very attractive, despite insufficient petals. Here is a welcome development and I hope more varieties along these lines will appear.

The greater majority of Roses become lighter in colour as the blooms open. One would like to see more varieties, especially among the H.T.s, where the colour intensifies as the flowers expand. McGredy's Sunset and Polly are examples among older varieties. The new hybrid musk Elmshorn also deepens in colour as the blooms age.

When are we going to get more Roses with really good keeping qualities, especially when one is forced to cut during a hot June? The answer may lie in stiffer petals, rather than the actual number, as singles like the old Karen Poulsen often keep longer than the full petalled hybrid teas. Among newer H.T.s I find the following last well, provided, and this is highly important, they are plunged immediately in water either overnight or far ot least six hours before arranging. Dr. Débat, Eden Rose, Golden Revelry, Gordon Eddie, Independence, Karl Herbst and Pink Spiral.

There are signs that the public is becoming less conservative regarding fragrance, realising that the so-called old-fashioned damask or otto of rose perfume is only one of the many different scents found in present day hybrid teas. I believe that an increasingly higher proportion of new introductions will be scented in varying degree and where fragrance is virtually absent, provided the variety is really good in other ways, no objections will be raised, even by the veriest beginner.

To return to colour. Are Rosarians less contemptuous regarding grey, lavender and allied colours ? I hope and believe there are great possibilities here. Grey Pearl was a preliminary step, very beautiful at times, but occasionally a dirty grey. There are now several H.T.s in this colour group under trial at Portadown, one not unlike Lavender Pinocchio, another a most attractive mauve which keeps its colour and lasts a week when cut.

The hybrid polyanthas, now classed in the new floribunda group, continue to make progress. There are still too many undistinguished pinks, though Mrs. Inge Poulsen and Ma Perkins are distinct, the former being creamy-pink, the latter more of a coral pink. I dislike varieties like Tantau's Delight with tightly packed blooms. August Seebauer, Commonwealth, Maid of Honour and Wilhelm Teetzmann are notable for proper spacing of individual flowers.

Cocorico is a very brilliant light scarlet which was badly needed, though in my garden it is not very free flowering. Reds in the same colour group as Independence may be expected and also more dark reds. (Dusky Maiden is a good variety but not free enough for my liking.) I have been disappointed with Poulsen's Crimson which never seems happy when cut. Tantau's Surprise and Red Favourite are promising. In the bright reds, Border King, Moulin Rouge and Siren appear outstanding.

Irene of Denmark, more dwarf in habit than the majority of floribundas, is good, though not a pure white, as there are slight pink flushes at times. It appears resistant to mildew. America has recently introduced White Pinocchio and Glacier, which should be worth a trial.

Yellow Pinocchio does well in my garden. The form is delightful, the buds being like miniature hybrid teas. This is really pinkish yellow and a pure yellow which holds its colour has still to appear—Goldilocks is the best yellow to date, but passes to cream.

No praise would be too high for Masquerade, the first really multi-coloured floribunda. This newcomer enjoys a definite wild Rose perfume, as do Fashion, Vogue and Yellow Pinocchio. Ma Perkins has an aroma suggesting honey. Chaperon Rouge, described as purple-red, is also said to have a very sweet fragrance, but has apparently not reached this country. It would seem that fragrance is gradually coming into this group, beginning with a somewhat subtle type of scent !

The new Dutch varieties Pompon Beauty and Signal Red, constitute a break in respect of form. Unfortunately, Signal Red seems to fade somewhat at times, though both tolerate dry weather with little discomfort. I believe that they are preliminary steps towards something better, as with Grey Pearl.

Wilhelm Kordes has produced several useful hybrids from Rosa moschata which make first rate specimen bushes. They show a wider colour range than the Pemberton Hybrid Musks, and appear highly resistant to disease. Flowering, especially in the case of Elmshorn, is continuous. Grandmaster is my favourite and is distinct in colour from other varieties in this group. Reddish apricot buds open to very large light apricot blooms. There is some fragrance, though personally I do not find the perfume very pronounced in any of the new moschata hybrids. As general utility Roses for thin soils, they can be highly recommended.

The × Kordesii climbers constitute a very promising development as little of real note has appeared among climbers and ramblers for many years. Final judgment must be deferred until the Trial Ground plants have been established for three or four years, but several Certificates have already been awarded. The claim that they are all perpetual flowering has yet to be proved, but they appear to be far less leggy at the base than the older climbers. This is a great advantage, as the climbing hybrid teas need plenty of space and horizontal training to secure best results, which is often impracticable in a small garden. The ideal is surely a variety that flowers freely and continuously from top to bottom and covers an eight foot larch pole without the necessity of waiting for blooms from lateral and sub-lateral growths.

Miniature Roses for rockeries, edgings and pot culture include some first class varieties and should become increasingly popular, provided they do not exceed twelve inches in height. Josephine Wheatcroft (syn. Rosina), Perle de Montserrat and similar introductions are excellent. Pigmy Gold is a new seedling from E. S. Boerner, raiser of Fashion, Masquerade, Vogue and other outstanding post-war floribundas, which grows about ten inches tall. As seen growing this is most impressive, but whether it is continuous like the miniature Chinas already mentioned, remains to be seen.

MY PROBLEM

W. WEST, Harlington, Middlesex

AS readers will probably guess, these notes were inspired by the book-marker which in recent years has accompanied the Annual. This book-marker was a happy thought, for it reminds Members of the object of our Society in a few simple but well-chosen words. " To spread the knowledge and love of the Rose." Only I would put " love " first, for given love, knowledge must surely follow. My love for the Rose was inspired by a Common Moss in my father's garden ; twenty-five years later, the sight of a Standard tree in full bloom made me determine to have a Rose garden, however small, of my own. Then commenced the period of learning, and, after twenty years, I am still gathering knowledge, a knowledge which brings an ever-increasing joy into Rose-growing. I remember how, after planting my first two dozen bushes, I spent a whole winter impatiently awaiting their flowering. I recall my pleasures and disappointments, my grievous losses, the times when I almost gave up rose-growing altogether. But all the time I was learning, and now, looking back, I know it was all worth while.

As knowledge increased, the standard of cultivation automatically improved, and my small garden commenced to fill with Roses. But I was separated from them by long hours spent at a desk and in travelling to and from my place of business, so, with an indifference to sartorial or any other considerations which I still feel, I started the habit of wearing a freshly-cut Rose in my button-hole every day between mid-May and early October. This habit started because I loved Roses, but I soon found I was also playing a small part in the work of the Society. I was, in fact, holding a daily Show, a Show of one bloom, and I can claim, in all humility, that because of it many Roses are at this moment growing where Roses did not grow before, and their owners are experiencing the joys which only Rose-growing can bring.

Picture the scene in a small suburban garden every morning after breakfast. The writer, assisted by his wife, selects a Rose with as much if not greater care than he shaves. Let me see, what did I wear on Monday ? Mme. Butterfly. Yesterday ? Phyllis Gold. Then it is the turn of a red. There's a likely Christopher Stone.

No, a trifle too far advanced—only a trifle, but it must be in as good condition for the 7.2 train in the evening as for the 8.3 in the morning. Ah ! Here's a Dr. Chandler that's just right. Reverently the flower is cut together with a leaf-stalk from which the two bottom leaves are removed, and leaves and bloom carefully inserted in the holder. Then a peep into the mirror before leaving for the station, not at the face or the thinning hair, but at the Rose now in my jacket. Vanity ? Of course, but there's a bit more to it than that.

People on the way to the station, many more on the train and the underground, colleagues in the office, workmen and girls in the factory—all will see that flower. So, for the glory of the Rose, the honour of the Society, the harmless vanity of the wearer, it must be good. How often am I asked, " What is the name of that one ? " Follows a sniff, and the exclamation, " What a beautiful Rose ! "

And so the work of spreading the love of the Rose goes on.

And the knowledge ? Well, my little daily Show has to have its Advisory Service, for many are the questions I am asked. Pruning, Pests, Diseases, Soil, Varieties. I answer faithfully, eagerly, from the knowledge gained through the years, and, remembering our book-marker, mention the debt I owe the Society of which I am proud to be a Member.

Of course it is not exactly easy to provide a perfect bud each day for nearly five months, especially as I dislike wearing a particular variety, or even colour, twice in one week. Quite a lot of bushes are needed. Actually I cut my button-holes from about 200 Hybrid Teas, of which over 60 are Standards, the number of varieties being 31. I am very fond of the Standard, partly because I am tall and stout, but also because it generally gives more blooms. Moreover, certain varieties seem to be more successful when grown in this way, at least in my garden. I am thinking particularly of Etoile de Hollande, Barbara Richards, and Ophelia, but there are others.

I do not wish to give the impression that I grow Roses only to provide myself with a daily button-hole, but I admit that all but one of my 31 varieties have the button-hole qualities, a shapely bud, good colour, *and* scent. In all humility, I submit that scent gives a Rose warmth. Many varieties are beautiful even though devoid of perfume, but they can find no place in my garden. Except Ena Harkness. Ena I must have, though in spite of the asterisk in the

Analysis, I have been unable to detect any perfume in this Rose except after heavy rain, and then it is what Mr. Harvey calls "elusive." But I go on trying. Ena grows in a narrow bed on one side of the path leading to my front door, four healthy Standards and three even healthier bushes, scarcely ever without blooms, and it has become a habit to sniff at one or more of them during the short walk from gate to door. A wonderful Rose, yet it is the only one of my little collection that is never considered for a button-hole.

Before concluding these notes I must complain that I am often asked an unfair question—What is my favourite variety ? I invariably reply that our Society treats the Nurserymen with twelve times as much consideration, but as I write these words in a little room overlooking my garden, I pause and my eye wanders over the superb Crimson Glory, the almost black Charles Mallerin, past Red Ensign, and stops at a small square bed where I see four Standards and four Bushes growing strongly and happily. Year after year this small bed gives a never ending display of gloriously coloured, sweetly scented Roses of perfect form and often of large size, and asking little, so very little, in return. Moderate, common-sense pruning, a sprinkling of potash and bone-meal, water once a week during dry spells, and love—above all, love. The colour ? " Salmon Pink, shaded Gold," says the Select List, but the bud has Carmine in it, too, making it glow like a very red sunset. Then I call to mind one dull evening when, after a particularly trying day, I entered my dining-room weary and depressed only to stop and gaze, spellbound, at the side-board. For there stood a vase of six of this same Rose, newly opened, illuminating the dark room with a blaze of light and colour and filling it with fragrance. I turned to my wife, who said, simply, "I thought you'd like it." Like ! My weariness and depression had vanished as if by magic. I felt a new man.

Yet when I go through the Analysis I never see the name, and I fear that the respected authorities who compile the Tables do not think so highly of this Rose as I do, though two or three Nurserymen list it among their twelve favourite varieties. I can only conclude my judgment is at fault, but whether this is so or not, every day of my life I thank the Maker of all Roses and the distinguished House of McGredy for giving me Hector Deane.

(Hector Deane is included in the new edition of "Roses: A Select List and Guide to Pruning," and has made a "come back" into this year's Analysis.—*Ed.*)

ROSES IN MOROCCO

MAJOR F. H. MELLOR

MANY people imagine that Morocco is a desert, though in actual fact the large fertile area between the Atlas mountains and the sea is carpeted with flowers in springtime. Wild Roses grow in profusion near the river valleys, their petals being sometimes used as a substitute for mint in Moorish tea.

At Marrakesh, in Southern Morocco, Monsieur Pierre Maillard has a large Rose nursery. He is a former pupil of Monsieur Meilland and grows many of the new varieties, notably those introduced by that famous French expert. The climate and conditions at Marrakesh are most suitable for this purpose and M. Maillard's bushes give great satisfaction to his clients in Tangier, many of whom are British.

In Meknes floribundas have been planted *en massif* in the squares with splendid results, while the Tangier administration, on the suggestion of a member of the National Rose Society, is trying out hybrid teas in the Place de France.

As far as Tangier is concerned, we prune at any time between the end of September and the New Year. I, personally, stagger my pruning, with the result that I have Roses in bloom from Christmas until about the 15th June. After that the heat is too great for all my varieties except Rouge Meilland (Happiness) which goes grandly on, producing fine blooms.

Roses make tremendous growth and need severe pruning, as otherwise they are smashed by the strong winds and make far too much wood.

Among red varieties, Rouge Meilland is quite outstanding here. Very vigorous, with well-shaped sun-proof blooms standing as erect as lances, I am surprised that it is not better liked in England. Perhaps I am hitting the mark when I suggest it is because this Rose likes sun and heat.

Charles Mallerin is as popular here as elsewhere, but does not like the sun, while I must reserve my opinion of Ena Harkness which, introduced into several gardens this year, has not started well. Alsace, Virgo, Mme. L. Dieudonné are all good Roses but Provence, orange yellow, introduced by Paolino in 1945, seems to me quite outstanding from every point of view. Lady Sylvia, surely the most perfectly shaped of all Roses, is a certain winner in the early spring before the sun destroys her lovely colouring.

This has been a good year. No mildew, no black-spot and only a little rust. Indeed, Roses do not suffer much from disease, though we have to fight a vigorous war against flying beetles which in some seasons play havoc with white and pink varieties.

To turn from hybrid teas to floribundas, I can say they are becoming as popular here as everywhere else. They bloom consistently for about nine months in the year and are quite at home. The other day I saw in a local garden two hundred Alain grown *en massif* and the effect was remarkable, though I preferred fifty Cocorico, with their upright growth and brilliant colour, in a smaller bed.

We are fortunate in Tangier, which was known to the ancients as the Garden of the Hesperides, for there can be no dispute that Roses really flourish in spite of the misdeeds of Moorish gardeners. Those of us who are members of the National Rose Society do all we can to spread the love and knowledge of the Rose and interest is steadily increasing. The British Flower Show is, alas, no longer held, but one day, I hope in the not far distant future, we shall have an International Flower Show.

N.B.—Any member of the National Rose Society visiting Tangier would be cordially welcomed by Major Mellor at his Office, "The Tangier Gazette," Rue du Statut, and he will be glad to assist them in any way possible during their visit.—*Ed.*

¶ The Publications Committee and the Hon. Editor desire to express their sincere thanks to all those friends who have assisted in the compilation of this 1953 Rose Annual.

LET THE RAMBLERS RAMBLE

S. A. PEARCE, Deputy Curator, Royal Botanic Gardens, Kew

I WONDER how many Rosarians, particularly those who only grow Rambler Roses in the conventional manner over an archway or on a pillar, have considered the possibilities of other and more or less unrestricted methods of growing these Roses. Many of our popular varieties and in particular those of extra vigour provide great possibilities where space is not definitely the deciding factor.

Whilst the majority of the Rambler varieties respond admirably to the common practice of drastic annual pruning to keep them within certain limits of the space available and when so treated provide a display almost unequalled by any other shrubby climber, often better and much more natural effects may be obtained by letting the growths develop more or less naturally and really ramble. By this I do not in any way suggest that the growths should be allowed to wander about in any desired direction, or become a source of annoyance by blocking a path or view, because much more than this can be achieved if the planting position is given careful consideration in the first place. If the growths of one of the strong growing Ramblers is allowed to wander over and amongst the branches of certain evergreen or deciduous trees, such as Holly, Thorn or an old Apple tree, one of the most spectacular floral displays of the whole year is provided. When allowed to " ramble " in this way the full beauty and natural grace of these Roses is really seen to the best advantage and fully appreciated. Again, certain unsightly buildings may be effectively screened by the use of Rambler and other climbing Roses when they are allowed to grow with reasonable freedom over and around them.

During a visit to a north Hampshire village during the summer of 1952, the writer viewed with great admiration a large specimen of that delightful variety Albertine, which had been most effectively used to cover a lean-to building at the side of a cottage. Although there were other examples of bedding and pillar Roses in the garden and all extremely well grown, they could in no way compare with the wonderful specimen of Albertine, which had been allowed to develop naturally and covered almost completely the whole roof and side of the building. When seen the Rose was in full bloom and a more delightful picture would have been hard to find anywhere. There were other pleasing examples of free and more or less unrestricted growing Ramblers in the same district. One which must be mentioned was a large specimen of Dorothy Perkins which had been planted at the base of an old Apple tree some fifteen feet high and into the branches of which the long growths of the Rose had grown and were sending out secondary arching shoots bearing masses of flowers. It was certainly one of the most striking displays of this variety that I have seen.

It is of interest here to call attention to the illustration in the Rose Annual for 1946 of a "Roadside Hedge," at Wembley. Miss P. M. Brown, in her accompanying note, wrote in praise of the variety Dr. van Fleet, when used for forming a hedge and at the same time allowed to ramble in a nearby tree of *Malus Elyii.* The photograph clearly portrayed the beauty of this variety when allowed this freedom of growth and gave ample proof of the possibilities of using such varieties for the purpose of forming a screen or hedge.

At Kew, the various varieties of climbing and Rambler Roses and also certain of the species, have for many years been grown in a number of ways and for different purposes. Perhaps one of the most effective spots in the gardens during mid-summer is the Rose Dell. Here many varieties of climbing Roses are planted in groups and allowed to grow freely over a framework of tree boughs to provide delightful features when in full flower. There are examples of strong growing species, such as Rosa moschata the "Musk Rose," and Rosa Soulieana rambling amongst the branches of nearby Holly trees. Other strong-growing hybrids and in particular the varieties Silver Moon, Alida Lovatt, Purity and Chaplins Pink Climber grow in profusion over portions of tree trunks and branches. Other varieties form bower-like groups when merely supported on the cut, forked branches of trees—the varieties Minnehaha, Goldfinch, Hiawatha, Seagull and Crimson Conquest, to mention but a few, all provide a most charming effect when in flower. The tumbling masses of bloom provide a floral feast that no words of mine can adequately describe.

In addition to the Rose Dell and the Rose Pergola, Rambling Roses are used at Kew to overhang and furnish the terrace walls of the pond in fromt of the Palm House. The varieties Thelma and the New Dawn are very accommodating with their long trailing growths tied down to a single wire running along the wall about three feet above the water level. Other secondary growth is allowed to grow and ramble at the top of the wall, so that in summer when the Roses are in flower a most pleasing and satisfying picture is presented. Finally, the value of Ramblers as Bedding Roses, used to fill large beds on the lawn, does not seem to be appreciated, possibly because the flowering season is not so extended as with the hybrid tea types. Nevertheless, certain varieties planted in large beds with the growths pegged and tied down to a height of about two feet above ground level do make a fine display when in flower. It would be nice to see this method of growing Rambler and Climber Roses more widely adopted in our public parks and gardens where ample space is available for the necessary large beds. At Kew, several large circular beds near the Temperate House are devoted to " pegged down " Ramblers, the varieties being Thelma, Alida Lovatt, Crimson Glow and Ruth Alexander. These beds provide popular features when in flower and the maintenance except for judicious annual pruning and tying down is negligible.

ROSE PURITY IN THE DELL, KEW GARDENS

ROSA COOPERII

ROLAND E. COOPER

"THE large and interesting collection of Rose species gathered together by the late Mr. Courtney Page at the N.R.S. Trial Ground is always worth a visit." So wrote Mr. Edward A. Bunyard in 1937 in the *New Flora and Silva*, and he goes on : " When I arrived in June, one Rose was outstanding—that grown under the name of 'Cooper Burmah.' It was then over 12 feet high. The flowers are white, about 4-5 inches in diameter, the foliage is a dark brownish green which it keeps all the winter. It is best described as a smaller laevigata and may be a hybrid of this with R. gigantea." R. gigantea is a variety of R. odorata but has normally creamy white flowers, but sometimes has blush to pale pink flowers and is then R. odorata v. crubescens. The late Mr. Page considered the Rose to be distinctive enough to have a name of its own and called it R. cooperii.

In the Botanic Garden at Maymyo, Burma, there was a fine R. gigantea which grew beside a spring and was trained on trellis all about it to appease the water spirits of the Burmese. Consequently, since plant news gets far abroad, the Political Agent of Sikkin a few years after 1922 heard of this plant and wrote to Burma for cuttings of it. Lengths of wood suitable for cuttings were made and some dipped several times in clayey mud and others with their ends stuck in potatoes were despatched from the coolness of the Shan Hills (4,000 feet) to the heat of Rangoon, across the Bay of Bengal to Calcutta, up the Himalayas by railway to Darjeeling and thence by runner to the Residency of the Political Officer in Gantok, the capital of Sikkin. But the P.O. had gone on a trip to Lhassa in course of his duties and his post followed him to Lhassa, the capital of Tibet. Here the parcel was opened and its contents mentioned to the Dalai Lama in conversation. His Eminence was given a few of the scions, for he likes flowers and all Roses are beautiful, and the P.O. returned to Seldain with the rest. He put them into the ground and they struck and grew, and this says much not only for their packing (newspaper and brown paper, both porous materials), but also for the vitality of the plant whose cuttings can go all the way from Maymyo to Lhassa and back to Gantok, from sea level to 15,000 feet, and still grow. A year or two afterwards the

P.O. again visited Lhassa and was shown with pride a flourishing plant which had arisen from the cuttings left at Lhassa. How is that for plant distribution ?

R. cooperii is very closely related to R. gigantea and was sent home among the seed collected by a native expedition to Mount Victoria in that country between 1922 and 1927, and so became associated with the man who organised the expedition and sent the seed home from Rangoon. The seed sent home from Mount Victoria was distributed from Cornwall and, when stationed in Edinburgh, I came across a plant of this Rose in the Royal Botanic Garden, but the weather was too hard for it to grow properly and show its true beauty. It had been given no name, having only staggered along since it germinated.

Roses of some kind or another are grown in every country where we have interest, officers and settlers. It is amusing sometimes to see how the cultural treatment needed in Britain is followed in climates far removed and very unlike ours, simply because " that is how they are treated at home " and, incidentally, it is amazing to see what disturbances Roses can take in their stride and survive.

It is our practice to prune our Roses as they are about to break into growth (bushes not climbers) after the dormant cold period of winter.

In Burma where the colder season runs from the month of September to February this is the time when Roses flourish and the time to grow the home bedding annuals. As the weather gets hotter so plant life's activities tend to get slower. This slowdown resembles our " dormancy " period because after the hottest weather the " rains " come in June and life stirs to new endeavour.

It would seem that the time to prune Rose bushes would be, if the basic practice of this country is to be followed, in the dormant growth period which is before the break of the rains. By doing this the plants which are in full flower at Christmas and New Year are not checked but allowed to continue flowering until the hot weather slows them down.

But the native gardener, knowing, I suppose, how slavishly many of his Sahibs stick to their own country routine, treats his Sahib's Roses also " à la sahib country."

What happens is incredible. The Rose bushes in full flower are dug up in mid January and laid in the sun to " make them go to sleep, so that they may be pruned." That is what the native gardener says and does and when asked why he bestows this rather terrible-to-look-at treatment, replies, "That is the English custom." Roses thus treated during their growing season do not all die but keep sufficient life in their pruned tissues to keep them going until the "rains" let them convalesce and come away again. So much is, or was, this the custom that when the Superintendent of the Botanic garden at Maymyo declined to dig up his Roses, dry them off for a sunny day and replant them when they were in full flower, but let them go on flowering until the hot season made them stop growing and then pruned them, he was considered "one of these newcomers who doesn't know our ways out here," and an even madder sahib than the rest, for he pruned his Roses at the time of the year when the sun was strongest, a time when no one does any work in the garden until the rains break in maybe a matter of a few days' time.

But the bush Roses grow and, to a surprising extent, flourish.

INTERNATIONAL AWARDS TO NEW ROSES, 1952

All America Rose Selections

Chrysler Imperial, H.T., raised by Dr W. E. Lammerts.
Ma Perkins, Hyb. Poly., raised by E. S. Boerner.

International Rose Trials at Geneva

Gold Medal, Buccaneer, H.T., raised by H. C. Swim.
Gold Medal, Moulin Rouge, Hyb. Poly., raised by Francis Meilland.
Certificate, Flambée, Hyb. Poly., raised by Charles Mallerin.
Certificate, Climber, Cl. Michèle Meilland, raised by Francis Meilland.
Certificate, Climber, Record, raised by Francis Meilland.

International Rose Trials at Rome

Gold Medal, Favorita, H.T., raised by E. S. Boerner.
First Certificate, Buccaneer, H.T., raised by H. C. Swim.
Second Certificate, Moulin Rouge, Hyb. Poly., raised by Francis Meilland.

The awards at Bagatelle, Paris, are given on page 48.

THE PRUNING TRIALS AT OAKLANDS

OBSERVATIONS on the first year :

From time to time there is considerable discussion on the pros and cons of *long* and *hard* pruning. In 1950 the Trial Ground Committee, at the request of the Publications Committee, planted a number of trees for pruning observation in order to make a factual report on the results.

Five plots were set aside and in each plot six trees each of Crimson Glory, Phyllis Gold and The Doctor, two feet to two feet six inches apart, were planted. In early March, 1951, all plants were moderately pruned except those in plot No. 1. These were left untouched and in subsequent years were to be " neglected."

For subsequent reference the terms " hard," " moderate " and " light " pruning are defined briefly as follows :

Hard.—Dead and decadent wood cut out and all healthy stems cut to the third or fourth eye (one which is pointing outward) from the base. (Decadent wood means a stem or part of a stem that has not thrown out a good shoot from the previous year's pruning cut.)

Moderate.—All thin twiggy growth and crossing stems removed, dead and decadent wood cut out, and the remaining sound and healthy shoots cut to about half the length of the previous year's growth to a bud pointing in a desired direction.

Light.—Same as moderate but the sound and healthy previous year's growth finally cut to the first or second eye (which is pointing in a desired direction) below the flowering footstalks.

On November 30th, 1951, the plants in plot No. 2 were *moderate* pruned.

In early March, 1952, the plants in plot No. 3 were *hard* pruned, in plot No. 4 were *light* pruned and in plot No. 5 *moderate* pruned.
Observations :

On June 17th, 1952, in plot No. 1 (neglected) there was a lot of dead wood, the plants were growing well and there was plenty of new growth from the base. The plants of The Doctor averaged 13 open flowers, six buds. The other varieties in similar proportions.

Plot No. 2 (moderate pruned November 30th). Crimson Glory growth poor ; two plants looked ill, but this may have been due to other unidentified causes. The other plants were average. Plants of The Doctor averaged six open flowers, three buds. Other varieties similar.

Plot No. 3 (hard pruned). Two or three shoots only to each plant, growing well, but no new growth from the base. The plants of The Doctor averaged five buds, no open flowers. Other varieties similar.

Plot No. 4 (light pruned). Growth very good, especially Phyllis Gold ; most plants had good new growth from the base. Plants of The Doctor averaged 19 open flowers, two buds. The flowering was well advanced. This plot gave the best general impression, and had many large and first class quality " exhibition " blooms.

Plot No. 5 (moderate pruned). Growth good, but little new growth from the base. Plants of The Doctor averaged six open flowers, six buds. In general the growth was less advanced than plot No. 2, and the quality of the flowers no better than on plot No. 4.

On September 10th observation showed that on plot No. 1 there was a large amount of dead wood and some of the plants were riddled with disease, The Doctor being almost defoliated by Black Spot. There was little flower and many heps ; in general the plants had grown well up to early August, and were now a tangled " jungle " with much unhealthy looking growth. The Black Spot disease was spreading from this plot down the line of the others, the infection gradually getting less as the plants were further away, plot No. 5 being scarcely touched. In all plots The Doctor was the worst affected, but Crimson Glory very little except in plot No. 2 (the nearest to the source of infection). In view of this the committee decided that the nearest six plants (The Doctor) should be taken up and destroyed in order to make a wider gap between plots Nos. 1 and 2. Also that on November 30th the plants may not have been sufficiently dormant and that in 1953 plot No. 2 should be pruned in January, the other plots as before in early March.

On plot No. 2 three plants were dead ; but as said before, this may have been and was probably due to other unidentified causes. The other plants had grown well, and the second flowering was at about the same time as on plot No. 4 ; there was a fair amount of new growth from the base.

Plot No. 3 looked well and had grown well but sparsely (few shoots), there was very little new growth from the base, the blooms had been good but comparatively few ; their best period had been at the end of June, about ten days later than plots Nos. 2, 4 and 5.

Plot No. 4.—The general effect was outstandingly the best, and there was ample new growth from the base, more than on any of the other plots. The first flowering was with plot No. 2 the earliest, and throughout the season the quantity of flowers had been higher and the quality as good as those on any other plot.

Plot No. 5 had caught up with plot No. 2 and looked about the same in all respects.

The soil at the Trial Ground is a rich heavy loam with gravel, well cultivated and sufficiently manured at the time of preparation. It has a small proportion of free calcium carbonate and has a *p*H of about neutral. The situation is nowhere protected and is open to all the wind and weather from the north-west to north-east. Under the conditions of the trial, it was evident that in this first year of the experiment the light pruning gave the best results, blooms as good in quality as any, and many more of them.

In conclusion it must be emphasised that the observations apply to *these* varieties, *these* plants and *these* particular conditions. In other conditions and in other circumstances it cannot be said that similar pruning might not give different results.

B. P.

¶ It is hoped that all members will endeavour to introduce friends and Rose lovers to the Society, for it is only by a still greater increase in our numbers that we can continue to provide the services that we are now doing.

¶ Unfortunately many of the back numbers of the Rose Annual are now exhausted, but the newer members are continually asking for them. The Secretary therefore would be grateful if members would return to him any copies that can be spared or are no longer required, sending them by carrier or passenger train carriage forward.

¶ Books on loan from our Library are very much in demand, and consequently many of them are showing evidence of continual use. Most of these books are now out of print and can only be replaced from second-hand sources. The Society would therefore be very grateful for the gift of any books on Rose subjects.

THE PRUNING TRIALS AT OAKLANDS.

Plot No. 1 "Neglected."

Plot No. 3 "Hard pruned."

Plot No. 4 "Light Pruned."
(Some flowers were over.)

Plot No. 5 "Medium Pruned."

Average plants of The Doctor, photographed on June 17th.

IRENE OF DENMARK. Floribunda (hyb. poly.)
Raised by Svend Poulsen, Denmark. Distributed by Sam McGredy & Son, Portadown.
First Class Trial Ground Certificate.

THE TRIAL GROUND

H. EDLAND

PERHAPS it is as well to commence this report with a reference to the Rose season of 1952 which I think, taken as a whole, cannot be said to have been a good one for Roses, as after a promising start it rather petered out. The first crop of bloom was good, in fact in many areas outstanding, but the later crops were below standard. The reason for this was the long periods of drought during the Summer months, and when eventually we had the rain it was accompanied by wintry cold and gales. This sadly interfered with the prospects to which all had looked forward of a good Autumn display.

Despite the bad flowering season, however, the trees at St. Albans grew well, and it was particularly pleasing to see them so effectively withstanding the drought. Looking at them on one occasion during this time, I was reminded of the comment which has so often been made to me by Mr. W. E. Harkness when discussing Roses (not an uncommon thing among Rose lovers !)—" Cultivation, my boy, cultivation, that's the answer " ; and it truly is the answer. The Rose foreman, too, must have been much gratified at the behaviour of the trees and felt rewarded for his hard work in the initial preparation of the beds. It is no light job to manually double dig an average of six new beds every year, each bed measuring some 120 feet long by 6 feet wide !

Disease started earlier than usual due to the abnormal heat during April and May, but fortunately the Copper White Oil Emulsion spray used at the Trial Ground kept it well under control. There was a moderate amount of Black Spot, but the main trouble, as in 1951, was Mildew. The spray was used seven times in all, against the various outbreaks. It was not indiscriminately used on all trees, as remedial and not preventive spraying is the policy of the Committee, it being an important aspect of the trials to discover the susceptibility of varieties to disease. A point worth recording in connection with the spraying was that the Copper White Oil Emulsion was first used at half strength, later going on to full strength. The reason for this was due to reports of some foliage damage elsewhere from the use of this spray. The Committee can confirm that it was quite effective in the Trial Ground against both Black Spot and Mildew, and that neither at half strength nor at full strength were there any instances of foliage damage.

In regard to the trials, Moulin Rouge was considered the outstanding Rose of the year, as it went on to the Autumn Show to win The President's International Trophy, a new award for the best New Seedling Rose of the year. The idea of the award emanated from the desire to encourage raisers and at the same time indicate the best variety. The winner was a worthy one this year, but it does not follow that it will automatically work out this way every year, one of the conditions governing the award being that the Rose must be exhibited at the Autumn Show. As can be realised the weather or the impossibility of a foreign raiser to stage his variety, may on occasion rule out a possible winner. Conditions last Autumn were adverse to the showing of full petalled Roses, consequently four eligible Hybrid Tea varieties—Bacchus (Gold Medal winner) from A. Dickson and Sons, Ltd., Brilliant (Gold Medal winner), from W. Kordes, Fred Howard, from Howard and Smith, and Fred W. Alesworth, from Herbert Robinson, were unable to be shown or were passed over through not being in good condition. The winner was a hybrid polyantha, as is Masquerade, the runner-up.

The excellent article by Wilhelm Kordes in the 1952 Rose Annual, giving his experiments in winter hardiness, created much anticipatory interest in the behaviour of some 40 of his climbers planted during the previous winter. In one particular, that of their colouring, they are beautiful. Although it is a little early yet to evaluate their other qualities, I must admit a little disappointment in that but few bloomed after the first flowering. However, this may be hasty judgment as with time to become established they may prove more remontant. It is also rather difficult for the time being to say how they shall be classified. Some give the impression of being best grown as large specimen bushes, whilst others appear to have a creeping habit ; the only thing is to wait and see. Referring again to their best quality, that of colour, many were most pleasing in shades ranging from pink to scarlet, together with others of a lemon yellow. The majority of the respective varieties carry fairly large blooms of 18 to 30 petals, and in addition many are fragrant. There is no doubt that some of them will oust from favouritism many of the old ramblers, particularly if they prove their hardiness and resistance to disease. So far they have done the latter, as in a bad year for Mildew they have been remarkably clean. This last winter will have provided a further test. I would mention that it may be some years before any reach the market, as obviously only a selection of the more perpetual flowering varieties are likely to be propagated for distribution.

Here I think I might interpose reference to the change in the pointing system. This is now as follows : Growth (Vigour, Habit and foliage) 20 points ; Freedom from disease 20 points ; Beauty of form, or formation of truss and colour 20 points ; Freedom of flowering 20 points ; Improvement on type 10 points, and Fragrance 10 points. The difference from former pointings will be noted is in the last two items. Fragrance, which hitherto commanded 20 points, has been halved to bring in " Improvement on type." Those who have a marked preference for fragrant Roses will possibly disagree with the new arrangement at first sight, but the Committee felt that, important though it may be, the award of a Certificate should not hinge on this one quality, as in the past was often the case. In comparison with growth, for example, half the number of points is a more reasonable assessment, as who would want a Rose, although fragrant, if it would not grow ? Similar comparison could be made with the other headings, and it is a fact that Roses combining the first four qualities and yet without fragrance have enjoyed long popularity. In other respects the same arrangement was continued as previously—a variety to gain a First Class Trial Ground Certificate has to obtain a minimum of 70 points out of the possible 100.

Throughout another season the Committee has had a difficult and long job in adjudicating upon the trees sent for trial, and I think it would not be out of place here for me, on behalf of the members, to pass on to the Committee the comments of appreciation received at the Society's headquarters. Without doubt the Committee consists of the best " Rose brains " in the country, and that they are willing to serve is a matter upon which the Society can congratulate itself. The knowledge too that one of them, our Hon. Editor, Mr. Bertram Park, has been honoured by the French Government, will also be of interest. Mr. Park has just been notified he is to receive a Medaille d'Honneur of the Decoration du Merite Agricole for the many years' service devoted to the " Society of Roses."

I will conclude this report with the usual, although none the less sincere, expression of thanks of the Committee to Mr. R. Line, Principal, and Mr. A. H. Lugg, Superintendent of The Institute of Agriculture, for their continued assistance throughout 1952. Also to Mr. Baines, our Rose foreman, for his devoted service.

LIST OF TRIAL GROUND AWARDS, 1952.

(To which is appended the Show Awards in 1952.)

BONNIE MAID (Hyb. Poly.). Trial Ground No. 616. Reg. No. 225. Raiser and Distributor E. B. Le Grice, North Walsham. A vigorous growing variety, with bronzy-green foliage *17*. Freedom from disease *15*. Semi-double blooms of 17 petals, 3 inches across produced in trusses. Colour carmine rose, can be likened to Dainty Maid with deeper colouring *16*. Freedom of flowering *15*. Fragrance *4*. Improvement on type *3*. Certificate of Merit Autumn Show, 1952.

BRILLIANT (H.T.). Trial Ground No. 375. Registered U.S.A. Poinsettia × Crimson Glory. Raiser W. Kordes. Distributors Wheatcroft Bros., Ltd., Ruddington. Free and upright growth, dark green foliage *17*. Freedom from disease *15*. Medium sized blooms of good shape, good for cutting, 34 petals, 4 inches when open. Colour deep scarlet *17*. Freedom of flowering *14*. Moderate fragrance *4*. Improvement on type *6*. Award withheld 1951 as variety not then named. Gold Medal Provincial Show, 1952.

DIAMOND JUBILEE (H.T.). Trial Ground No. 573. Registered U.S.A. Raiser E. S. Boerner, of Jackson Perkins Co., New York. Distributors Wood and Ingram, Huntingdon. A strong growing bushy variety, with dark green glossy foliage *18*. Freedom from disease *12*. Large well shaped very full blooms of exhibition size. Colour variable, at its best buff yellow, but inclined to come pale *15*. Freedom of flowering *12*. Fragrance *8*. Improvement on type *5*.

ETHEL SANDAY (H.T.). Trial Ground No. 577. Registration No. 288. Rex Anderson × Audrey Cobden. Raiser Oliver Mee, Wilmslow. Distributors John Sanday (Roses) Ltd., Bristol. Growth upright and vigorous, with abundant dark green foliage. Good habit *15*. Freedom from disease *15*. Blooms full and shapely, 40 petals. Colour yellow deepening to canary, flushed apricot *15*. Freedom of flowering *15*. Moderate fragrance *5*. Improvement on type *5*.

FANAL (Hyb. Poly.). Trial Ground No. 524. Registration No. 282. Raiser M. Tantau, Germany. Distributors Wheatcroft Bros., Ltd., Ruddington. A bushy compact grower of good habit, dark green large foliage *18*. Freedom from disease *18*. Semi-double deep pink blooms of 12 petals produced in trusses. Individual blooms 3½ inches across *15*. Freedom of flowering *15*. Slight fragrance *3*. Improvement on type *4*. Award withheld 1951 as variety not then named.

FANDANGO (H.T.). Trial Ground No. 493. Registered U.S.A. Charlotte Armstrong × Unnamed seedling. Raiser Herbert C. Swim, of Armstrong Nurseries, California. Distributors R. Harkness and Co., Hitchin. Growth upright and bushy with dark green leathery foliage *16*. Freedom from disease *13*. Blooms large but thin, 17 petals, 4½ inches when open. Colour scarlet shaded orange at base *17*. Freedom of flowering *14*. Moderate fragrance *5*. Improvement on type *5*.

FIGURINE (H.T.). Trial Ground No. 377. Registration No. 281. Soeur Thérèse × unknown seedling. Raisers Louis Lens, Ltd., Belgium. Vigorous growth with abundant dark green foliage *18*. Freedom from disease *15*. Blooms shapely of medium size, several together, 25 petals, colour china pink *14*. Freedom of flowering *15*. Moderate fragrance *5*. Improvement on type *5*. Award withheld 1951 as then not named.

FIRST LOVE (H.T.). Trial Ground No. 494. Registered U.S.A. Charlotte Armstrong × Show Girl. Raiser Herbert C. Swim, of Armstrong Nurseries, California. Distributors R. Harkness and Co., Hitchin. Growth vigorous and bushy, medium green foliage *17*. Freedom from disease *15*. Blooms medium size, well shaped but rather thin, 24 petals. Colour pale pink deepening in tone on edges of petals *12*. Freedom of flowering *16*. Moderate fragrance *5*. Improvement on type *5*. Certificate of Merit Autumn Show, 1952.

FRIEDRICH SCHWARZ (H.T.). Trial Ground No. 369. Registration No. 188. Poinsettia × (Crimson Glory × Lord Charlemont). Raiser W. Kordes, Germany. Distributors Wheatcroft Bros., Ltd., Ruddington. Upright vigorous growth, large dark green foliage *18*. Freedom from disease *12*. Blooms shapely and long pointed in bud, 3½ inches when open, 32 petals. Colour crimson with matt red on reverse *14*. Freedom of flowering *15*. Strong fragrance *10*. Improvement on type *8*. Certificate of Merit Autumn Show, 1951.

GERTRUD WESTPHAL (Hyb. Poly.). Trial Ground No. 710. Registration No. 193. Baby Chateau × R. rubiginosa magnifica. Raiser W. Kordes, Germany. Distributors Wheatcroft Bros., Ltd., Ruddington. Bushy compact habit, medium green foliage *14*. Freedom from disease *18*. Blooms orange-scarlet of 13 petals, approximately 3½ inches when open. Produced in well spaced trusses *16*. Freedom of flowering *17*. Fragrance *5*. Improvement on type *2*.

GRANDMASTER (Hyb. Moschata). Trial Ground No. 470. Registration No. 202. Raiser W. Kordes, Germany. Distributors Henry Morse and Sons, Norwich. A shrub variety, best lightly pruned. Foliage medium green and disease resistant *15*. Freedom from disease *18*. Semi-double blooms, 10 petals, produced in trusses. When open 2½ inches across. Colour apricot and lemon shaded pink *15*. Freedom of flowering *15*. Good fragrance *8*. Improvement on type *3*. Awarded Gold Medal Autumn Show, 1951.

KÄTHE DUVIGNEAU (Hyb. Poly.). Trial Ground No. 527. Registration No. 273. Raiser M. Tantau, Germany. Distributors Wheatcroft Bros., Ltd., Ruddington. Vigorous growth, medium green foliage *15*. Freedom from disease *18*. Attractive glowing scarlet blooms of 8 petals produced in trusses. Individual blooms 3 inches when open *14*. Freedom of flowering *16*. Moderate fragrance *5*. Improvement on type *3*.

MME. LOUISE LAPERRIÈRE (H.T.). Trial Ground No. 644. Registration No. 283. Raiser M. Laperrière, France. Distributors Wheatcroft Bros., Ltd., Ruddington. Compact bushy vigorous growth, dark green foliage *17*. Freedom from disease *17*. Full shapely blooms of medium size, 42 petals. Colour dark crimson *14*. (Very similar to Etoile de Hollande.) Freedom of flowering *16*. Strong fragrance *8*. Improvement on type *3*.

MAGALI (H.T.). Trial Ground No. 515. Registration No. 274. Charles P. Kilham × Brasier. Raiser C. Mallerin, France. Distributors Wheatcroft Bros., Ltd., Ruddington. A very vigorous growing variety with abundant dark green leathery foliage *20*. Freedom from disease *15*. Salmon pink blooms of 45 petals, rather loose petalled and globular *12*. Freedom of flowering *18*. Slight fragrance *2*. Improvement on type *3*.

MAID OF HONOUR (SCHLESWIG) (Hyb. Poly.). Trial Ground No. 468. Registration No. 203. Holstein × Crimson Glory. Raiser W. Kordes, Germany. Distributors Henry Morse and Sons, Norwich. Bushy growth, medium size dark green foliage *18*. Freedom from disease *14*. A single variety. Blooms opening to approximately 4 inches across, produced in trusses, colour salmon pink with paler centre *15*. Freedom of flowering *15*. Slight fragrance *3*. Improvement on type *5*. Certificate of Merit Summer Show, 1951.

MA PERKINS (Hyb. Poly.). Trial Ground No. 476. Registered U.S.A. Red Radiance × Fashion. Raiser E. S. Boerner, Jackson and Perkins Co., New York. Distributors S. McGredy and Son, Portadown, and Alex. Dickson and Sons, Belfast. Vigorous bushy habit, medium green foliage *15*. Freedom from disease *15*. Large full cup-shaped blooms, 3 inches when open, 32 petals. Produced several together. Colour pale pink, edges of petals deeper pink *15*. Freedom of flowering *15*. Good fragrance *8*. Improvement on type *8*. Certificate of Merit Summer Show, 1952.

MÄRCHENLAND (Hyb. Poly.). Trial Ground No. 525. Registration No. 235. Raiser M. Tantau, Germany. Distributors Wheatcroft Bros., Ltd., Ruddington. Vigorous and upright growth, bushy. Medium green glossy foliage *20*. Freedom from disease *15*. Blooms flat produced in clusters, 32 petals. Colour pale pink reverse deep pink. Similar to Dainty Maid but more petalage *15*. Freedom of flowering *20*. Fragrance *5*. Improvement on type *8*.

MOULIN ROUGE (Hyb. Poly.). Trial Ground No. 522. Registration No. 271. Alain × Orange Triumph. Raiser F. Meilland, France. Distributors Wheatcroft Bros., Ltd., Ruddington. A vigorous growing variety with medium green glossy foliage *16*. Freedom from disease *18*. Blooms of 18 petals, 2½ inches when open, produced in well spaced trusses. Colour bright glowing scarlet, most attractive *20*. Freedom of flowering *16*. Slight fragrance *2*. Improvement on type *5*. Gold Medal and President's International trophy, Autumn Show, 1952.

NYMPH (Hyb. Poly.). Trial Ground No. 579. Registration No. 258. Fashion × Unnamed seedling. Raisers and Distributors A. Dickson and Sons, Ltd., Belfast. Compact bushy growth, dark green glossy foliage *16*. Freedom from disease *16*. Double blooms of 48 petals produced in trusses. Individual blooms 2½ inches across when open. Colour coral salmon *12*. Freedom of flowering *15*. Slight fragrance *3*. Improvement on type *5*.

PLOMIN (Hyb. Poly.). Trial Ground No. 536. Registration No. 272. Raiser M. Tantau, Germany. Distributors Wheatcroft Bros., Ltd., Ruddington. Growth vigorous and bushy with small foliage of medium green *16*. Freedom from disease *15*. Blooms 3 inches when open of 20 petals produced in clusters. Colour creamy pink *12*. Freedom of flowering *18*. Moderate fragrance *5*. Improvement on type *8*.

RED FAVOURITE (Hyb. Poly.). Trial Ground No. 532. Registration No. 218. Raiser M. Tantau, Germany. Distributors Wheatcroft Bros., Ltd., Ruddington. Growth vigorous and bushy. Large medium green glossy foliage *15*. Freedom from disease *17*. Blooms of 12 petals, 2½ inches when open, produced in clusters. Colour dark crimson, a rather inadequate description as the blooms appear " alive " with an attractive glow *18*. Freedom of flowering *14*. Slight fragrance *2*. Improvement on type *5*. Certificate of Merit Provincial Show, 1951.

SIREN (Hyb. Poly.). Trial Ground No. 364. Registration No. 279. (Baby Chateau × Else Poulsen) × Independence. Raiser W. Kordes, Germany. Distributors Wheatcroft Bros., Ltd., Ruddington. Upright vigorous growth, dark green foliage *17*. Freedom from disease *15*. Blooms good form in bud borne in well spaced trusses, 22 petals, 2½ inches when open. Colour orange scarlet *18*. Freedom of flowering *18*. No fragrance. Improvement on type *2*. Award withheld 1951 as variety not then named. Gold Medal Provincial Show, 1952.

WILL SCARLET (Hyb. Moschata). Trial Ground No. 631. Registration No. 260. Sport of Wilhelm. Distributors T. Hilling and Co., Chobham, Woking. A vigorous growing shrub, foliage bronzy green *18*. Freedom from disease *18*. Semi-double blooms of 11 petals produced in clusters, individual blooms 2½ inches across. Colour scarlet *15*. Freedom of flowering *12*. Moderate fragrance *5*. Improvement on type *5*.

SHOW AWARDS, 1952.

Gold Medals were awarded to :—

BACCHUS (H.T.). Raisers and Exhibitors A. Dickson and Sons, Ltd., Belfast. Bright rose red. Blooms large and shapely, 25 petals. Sweetly fragrant. This would appear to be a good garden variety, the trees in the Trial Ground having grown well. The variety was awarded a Trial Ground Certificate in 1951. Trial Ground No. 305.

BRILLIANT (H.T.). For description see Trial Ground Awards.

MASQUERADE (Hyb. Poly.). Parentage Goldilocks × Holiday. Raised by E. S. Boerner, of Jackson and Perkins Company. Exhibitors S. McGredy and Son, Portadown, and A. Dickson and Sons, Ltd., Belfast. A very attractive bedding variety of bushy habit and with plentiful dark green foliage. Blooms produced in clusters of yellow, salmon pink and scarlet in separate colours on the same truss. Awarded a Trial Ground Certificate in 1951. Trial Ground No. 474.

MOULIN ROUGE (Hyb. Poly.). For description see Trial Ground Awards.

SIREN (Hyb. Poly.). For description see Trial Ground Awards.

Certificates of Merit were awarded to :—

BONNIE MAID (Hyb. Poly.). For description see Trial Ground Awards.

BORDER KING (Hyb. Poly.). Raised by G. de Ruiter. Exhibitors C. Gregory and Son, Ltd., Chilwell. Brilliant strawberry red blooms produced in clusters. Size when open 1¾ inches, 17 petals. A very vigorous growing variety with plentiful dark glossy green foliage. Awarded a Trial Ground Certificate in 1951. Trial Ground No. 326.

FIRST LOVE (H. T.). For description see Trial Ground Awards.

FRED W. ALESWORTH (H.T.). Poinsettia × Crimson Glory. Raised by Herbert Robinson, Hinckley. Exhibitors Bakers, Codsall, Wolverhampton. Deep crimson blooms, large and shapely. Sweetly fragrant. A vigorous growing and branching variety with dark green foliage. Trial Ground Certificate 1951. Trial Ground No. 273.

IRENE OF DENMARK (Hyb. Poly.). Mrs. Cutbush × Edina. Raised by Svend Poulsen, Denmark. Exhibitors S. McGredy and Son, Portadown. A white variety. Blooms freely produced in trusses. Individual blooms 2½ inches in diameter. Bushy compact vigorous growth. Trial Ground Certificate 1950. Trial Ground No. 349.

MA PERKINS (Hyb. Poly.). For description see Trial Ground Awards.

POULSEN'S SUPREME (Hyb. Poly.). Raised by Svend Poulsen, Denmark. Exhibitors S. McGredy and Son, Portadown. A rose pink coloured variety. Blooms small 2 inches in diameter when open produced in trusses, 8 petals. Growth upright and free. Trial Ground Certificate 1950. Trial Ground No. 196.

SALMON PERFECTION (Hyb. Poly.). Raised by G. de Ruiter, Holland. Exhibitors S. McGredy and Son. A salmon orange variety. Blooms of 25 petals small and cupped, 1½ inches diameter when open. Produced in trusses. Growth vigorous and bushy. Dark green leathery foliage. Trial Ground Certificate, 1950. Trial Ground No. 243.

YELLOW PINOCCHIO (Hyb. Poly.). Goldilocks × Marionette. Raised by E. S. Boerner, of Jackson and Perkins Co. Exhibitors S. McGredy and Son, Portadown. Yellow in bud changing to white with edge of pink. Blooms produced in clusters. Individual blooms 35 petals, opening to 2½ inches diameter. Growth compact and bushy. Abundant dark green foliage. Trial Ground Certificate, 1951. Trial Ground No. 475.

THE ARTISTIC CLASSES AT THE SUMMER SHOW

JULIA CLEMENTS

IT could clearly be seen when studying the exhibits in the artistic classes at the Summer Show of 1952 that the competitors are introducing more design into their arrangements, for most of the exhibits showed some personal distinction.

Of course, listening to the comments of some who do not understand the subject, you could hear such remarks as, " Who wants to see Roses arranged like that ? " and another, " But that's not natural, Roses do not grow like that." These comments, however, will not deter those who wish to arrange Roses artistically or according to some accepted principles of design, for it is the *creation of a design with Roses in a vase* that gives further pleasure to the person who may already have nurtured the growth of these lovely blooms.

And after all, although one is taught to follow as much as possible the feeling for a plant's growth when using it in design, one cannot always arrange flowers *as they grow*, for who would want to bring an eight foot tall dahlia into the drawing room, with the announcement, " That is how it grows."

I thought the exhibitors all showed a very good sense of colour combination and I particularly liked the arrangement of mauve and purple old-fashioned Roses which stood on a lime green cloth.

Another lovely table, although it did not win a prize, was made by Mrs. F. Barker. She used Picture Roses in a Victorian glass sugar bowl, arranged triangularly, and at each side stood a further low crescent arrangement of similar blooms. The whole stood on a cloth of pale cream lace with an underslip of the same colour as the pink of the Roses.

On the whole I thought there was a distinct improvement in the standard of artistic work shown ; now the competitors are looking forward to more exciting schedules.

Photograph by] [*Karminski*

An arrangement of Roses with " other decoration " by Mrs. Evan Jones, of Dorchester, at the " Evening News " Show, 1951.

(*See new Artistic Classes in the Show Schedules for 1953*).

An arrangement of Roses with Rose foliage by Mrs. Barker, of Colchester, at the National Rose Society's Summer Show, 1952.

By courtesy of] [*Jackson & Perkins Co., New York*

Fashion, arranged in an alabaster vase by Edna Whitsitt.

A NOTE FROM CANADA

FRANK FLETT, HAMILTON, CANADA

I HAVE been a member of the National Rose Society for about thirty years and have always looked forward with interest to receiving my copy of the " Annual " each year, but never expected to be called upon to make a contribution to its pages. However, I shall do the best I can with the hope that maybe someone will find something of interest in what I have to say.

The prime requisite in Rose growing, like everything else, is the proper spirit. Without that you are licked to start with. This is not the fervor which is aroused by viewing a beautiful Rose such as is seen at a show or even viewing a beautiful garden. It is rather the persistent enthusiasm which extends over the years, considering the Roses as your children and desiring to give them every possible opportunity to achieve their best.

This article will be restricted to local conditions necessarily as Canada is a very large territory, larger in fact than the United States. It stretches from the Atlantic to the Pacific, a distance of something like four thousand miles, and from the Great Lakes to the North Pole. It even contains the magnetic pole if that is any attraction.

Hamilton is in the most southern part of Canada, at the western end of Lake Ontario in the same latitude as the south of France. We have not a warm Mediterranean sea to the south of us to moderate the climate, although Lake Ontario is never frozen over in the winter. We can expect frost about the middle of October and it will continue off and on until about the middle of May. The winter temperature may go to zero at times, but we have warm days, of course, when the temperature is above freezing. It will drop as much as thirty degrees, sometimes, in as many hours. It is this thawing and freezing which is hard on Roses. March is particularly bad as it is freezing at night and thawing in the daytime. We cannot count on a blanket of snow for winter protection as it may lie for weeks, then all melt in a week, to be followed later by more snow. The average snowfall in Hamilton is 58 inches, but last winter we had 75.3 inches. Fortunately this is spread out over four months.

The choicest Roses are somewhat tender and it is advisable to protect these in winter. This can be accomplished by piling the earth up as high as circumstances will permit and filling in the hollows with animal manure, if you can get it, or rotted leaves will substitute. When the ground is permanently frozen and you think winter is really here, about the first of December, the Roses are covered over with leaves so that when settled these will be a foot or more thick. About the first of April this covering is removed and the Roses pruned. By this method winter loss is exceptional.

Not many standard or half standards are grown. They can be wintered satisfactorily by loosening the earth at one side and laying the stem flat on the ground, covering it with earth and leaves, or similar material. Some of the more tender climbers are taken down and covered with burlap or canvas.

Many Roses are planted in the spring, early in April being desirable but fall planting is to be preferred, about the latter part of October. This gives the roots a chance to take hold in the relatively warm soil. If fall planted, they should only be partially cut back but if spring planted then hard back. The bud should be not more than one inch below the ground.

Most of the Roses propagated in Canada are budded on multiflora and are pruned early in April. If well protected in the winter there will still be live wood to cut back or out, besides that killed by the frost. This year a friend and myself are experimenting with Mrs. Sam McGredy, by cutting out only the winter-killed wood. Another friend has several magnificent bushes of this variety, which are a picture in the fall and these have never been cut hard back.

Rose bushes can be obtained in many stores in the spring. Even hardware stores sell them. One department store is to be congratulated on the way they handle theirs. The hardware store treats them as if they were just another bolt. The greenhouses, who have been growing them all winter for cut flowers, sell a lot of them in the spring also. These are generally grafted plants on manetti. Unfortunately many of these are not dug but pulled up off the benches they have been grown on. One of the reasons they are disposed of is because they have midge in the house ; word of this later ! Nevertheless some good results can be had with these bushes if care is taken in the selection and they are hard pruned back at planting.

The hybrid tea type Roses bloom about the second or third week in June. The hybrid perpetuals are a little later. The H.T.s will continue to bloom intermittently all summer. There is generally quite a display again in late September or early October. We get some very fine specimens in the mellow days of October. We seldom get a hard frost before the latter part of October and quite a few blooms can even be cut in November of some seasons.

To get Roses earlier, I have a frame which I put over the ends of one of the beds. This is put up about the middle of November. It consists of four wooden sides long enough for two glass sashes over the top. There are two tea Roses in this which have been there for many years. The stems stay green to the tips. The frame is removed about the middle of May when the new shoots start hitting the glass. By this procedure the Roses bloom two weeks or more ahead of those not so treated.

We have Rose pests, too ! Leaf roller early in the spring, green fly, mildew and black spot. Green fly can be combated by hitting them with a nicotine spray. The mildew and black spot by dusting with nine parts dusting sulphur and one part arsenate of lead powder. You can get dusting sulphur so fine it will float like a fog on the air if there is no wind. Perhaps the reason the sulphur gets results here is because of our higher temperatures. 80°F. is a very common temperature in July and August. This is in the shade. In the sun it would be hotter.

Midge ! I understand you have not made its acquaintance in Britain. You should be thankful for that. It is a tiny fly which lays its eggs in a terminal shoot and when the young hatch they attack the minute flower bud and it turns black. You would think, if you did not know why, that the shoot was just blind. The maggots which are whitish about a tenth of an inch long, drop to the ground and pupate in the soil, emerging in a week or two to start their cycle over again. These can be controlled by dusting every ten days for three applications, at least, of five per cent. D.D.T.

We are all interested in new Roses and like to read about them in the catalogues. It is well, however, to pay particular attention to what they do *not* say about them. They describe their virtues but invariably omit their faults.

Ena Harkness must do better in Britain than any I have seen here. It has not many blooms here nor is it a very strong grower. Etoile de Hollande has proven one of our best reds. It will grow twice the height of Crimson Glory, which is a good grower also.

Generally speaking, the Roses which top the list in Britain do well here but with our warmer temperatures the blooms mature faster and the ones with fewer petals are very fleeting and are seen at their best only for a short while, except in our autumn.

Now for a word to the Canadian members who wish to import Roses from the old country. An import permit is necessary. This is obtained by applying to the Department of Agriculture at Ottawa. There is a regular application form to be filled out to obtain the permit. Small lots come across very well by mail. Order your bushes early for fall delivery. They ship better then. If they do not come in time to plant before the ground freezes up, keep them over until spring. Have a spot in the vegetable garden where it is relatively dry and cover it over with a thick coating of leaves or straw. When your bushes arrive and it is too late to plant, tie them in small bundles with a fair sized insulated wire. An old lamp cord will do. Have a stick at the end of the wire which should come above the earth. Put the bundles in flat, cover with earth, then with the leaves or straw. In the spring dig carefully around the bundles. The insulated wire will help you locate them. Order from a firm who not only can supply quality stock but also knows how to pack and ship over the ocean and also knows how to make out the necessary customs invoices and certificates. Insist on wooden labels.

A department store in this city some years ago ordered a shipment of Roses from Holland. The Dutchmen put paper labels on them which disintegrated on the long, moist journey over. The store hired a gardener to replace the labels. No wonder that Etoile de Hollande, if it grew, had pink flowers on it !

"*Eglentine semeth to have been firste called in Greek Kynorhodos, because the rote heled them that were bitten of a mad dogge.*"—

Turners Herbal, 1568.

THE ROSE ANALYSIS

H. EDLAND

IN response to the invitation of last year, three new contributors volunteered to help with the current Analysis, and I am sure all will subscribe to the expression of the thanks of the Publications Committee. If other members feel competent to tackle the job of completing the various lists, either in full or in part, their help too will be most welcome. In the main, the contributors were the same as in the past and in expressing thanks to the newcomers, the help of the former is not overlooked.

THE VOTERS

Amateurs.—E. H. Ackerman (Dorset), E. M. Allen (Devon), G. D. Burch (Bucks), S. Carson (Northumberland), G. W. Chadwick (Yorkshire), H. G. Clacy (Surrey), F. Fairbrother (Devon), J. N. Hart (Middlesex), N. P. Harvey (Kent), L. Hollis (Surrey), E. Royalton Kisch (Kent), M. L. Kemp (Essex), Oliver Mee (Cheshire), Mrs. Machin (Cheshire), A. Norman (Surrey), C. R. Nicholls (Salop), J. Roscoe (Lancs), W. J. W. Sanday (Somerset), W. H. Sumpster (Surrey), W. C. Thorn (Essex), C. F. Warren (Cheshire), R. White (Bucks).

Nurserymen.—J. H. Alexander (Midlothian), D. Bide (Surrey), J. A. Chatterton (Cheshire), G. Condliffe (Midlothian), Messrs. D. and W. Croll (Angus), A. Dickson (Ireland), C. J. Dillon (Northumberland), A. Fryer (Cheshire), G. Geary (Leicester), C. W. Gregory (Notts), W. E. Harkness (Herts), F. H. Hicks (Berks), W. Johnston (Ireland), L. C. Longley (Kent), J. Mattock (Oxon), A. J. Merryweather (Notts), E. H. Morse (Norfolk), A. E. Nevard (Essex), E. W. Stedman (Northamptonshire), A. R. Treseder (Glamorgan), H. Wheatcroft (Notts), H. Williamson (Herefordshire), F. G. Wollard-Letts (Suffolk).

The tables have been compiled as follows : First, each variety pointed according to the position it occupied in the voters' list, that is to say, if 24 varieties were asked for, the variety heading the list received 24 points, and so on down the scale to the last on the list which received one point. The points thus received by the respective varieties were then added together and the variety placed numerically in position in the tables.

In the list of " Large Specimen Blooms " and in that of " Roses for General Garden Cultivation " the varieties especially suitable as Standard Roses are marked with † and those with especially pronounced fragrance with *.

Separate tables for North and South in the Roses for General Garden Cultivation have been continued this year. The former procedure has been adopted of dividing the country with an imaginary line drawn across the map from Lowestoft to Bristol.

It is very pleasing to report that there has been less trouble generally from Black Spot this year, or so one would gauge from the lessening of correspondence on this subject. Most correspondents, however, concluded their letters with a request for a list of varieties immune to the disease. My reply had to be to the effect that although certain varieties are more resistant than others, the incidence of disease is very variable, and few H.T. Roses can be claimed to be entirely immune under conditions which favour the disease. It is always wise to take protective measures, if the disease should be found or if it has been prevalent in the garden the previous year, but attention is drawn to the article and illustrations on another page.

VARIETIES PRODUCING LARGE SPECIMEN BLOOMS

Table 1.—(Amateurs) **Table 2.—(Nurserymen)**

Position	NAME	Number of Points	Position	NAME	Number of Points
1	Peace	457	1	Peace	499
2	The Doctor	331	2	The Doctor	401
2	William Harvey	331	3	Glory of Rome...	366
4	Glory of Rome	297	4	Crimson Glory...	334
5	Red Ensign	294	5	William Harvey	326
6	McGredy's Yellow	291	6	McGredy's Yellow	308
7	Phyllis Gold	283	7	Ena Harkness	304
8	Barbara Richards	279	8	Barbara Richards	286
9	Ena Harkness	274	8	Red Ensign	286
10	Rex Anderson	273	10	Phyllis Gold	235
11	Directeur Guerin	236	11	Dame Edith Helen	226
12	Crimson Glory	228	12	Golden Dawn	200
13	Mrs. C. Lamplough	221	13	McGredy's Ivory	198
14	Sam McGredy	198	14	Golden Melody	159
15	McGredy's Ivory	186	15	Mrs. C. Lamplough	147
16	Show Girl	169	16	Rex Anderson	146
17	Karl Herbst	130	17	Show Girl	126
18	Golden Dawn	114	18	Mrs. A. R. Barraclough	120
19	Dame Edith Helen	113	18	Mrs. Henry Bowles	120
20	William Moore	95	20	Karl Herbst	117
21	Golden Melody	91	21	Symphonie	111
22	Symphonie	83	22	Dorothy Anderson	104
22	Dorothy Anderson	83	23	Sam McGredy	95
24	Charlotte Armstrong	77	24	Eden Rose	82

Table 3.—LARGE SPECIMEN BLOOMS

Position	Total No. of Points	Pointed by Amateurs	Pointed by Nurserymen	NAME	Date of Introduction	COLOUR
1	956	457	499	†Peace	1947	Golden yellow petals edged pink
2	732	331	401	*†The Doctor	1939	Bright silvery rose
3	663	297	366	*Glory of Rome	1937	Reddish pink
4	658	331	327	*William Harvey	1947	Dusky scarlet red
5	599	291	308	†McGredy's Yellow	1933	Pale yellow
6	580	294	286	*Red Ensign	1947	Deep crimson
7	578	274	304	*†Ena Harkness	1946	Rich glowing red
8	565	279	286	*†Barbara Richards	1930	Maize yellow, flushed rose
9	562	228	334	*†Crimson Glory	1935	Deep velvety crimson
10	518	283	235	†Phyllis Gold	1934	Golden yellow
11	419	273	146	Rex Anderson	1937	Cream shaded gold
12	368	221	147	Mrs. C. Lamplough	1920	Lemon white
13	354	156	198	McGredy's Ivory	1926	Creamy white shaded yellow
14	339	113	226	*Dame Edith Helen	1926	Pure glowing pink
15	314	114	200	*†Golden Dawn	1929	Pale lemon yellow
16	295	169	126	†Show Girl	1950	Deep pink
17	293	198	95	Sam McGredy	1937	Buff shaded cream
18	285	236	49	Directeur Guerin	1937	Creamy yellow, centre golden orange
19	250	91	159	*Golden Melody	1939	Buff yellow
20	247	130	117	Karl Herbst	1950	Scarlet
21	196	76	120	Mrs. A. R. Barraclough ...	1926	Carmine pink
22	194	83	111	Symphonie	1949	Carmine
23	187	83	104	Dorothy Anderson	1949	Bright rose pink
24	174	54	120	†Mrs. Henry Bowles	1921	Glowing rose

*The most highly fragrant varieties.
† The most suitable for standards.

ROSES FOR GENERAL GARDEN CULTIVATION

Table 4.—(Amateurs, North)

Position	NAME	Number of Points
1	Peace	174
2	Ena Harkness	170
3	McGredy's Yellow	114
4	Mrs. Sam McGredy	112
5	Picture	110
6	Golden Melody	87
7	Crimson Glory	86
8	Phyllis Gold	85
9	Etoile de Hollande	77
10	The Doctor	72
11	Comtesse Vandal	54
12	Madame Butterfly	51
13	President Herbert Hoover	46
14	Christopher Stone	45
15	Golden Dawn	42
16	Lady Sylvia	39
16	Mrs. Henry Bowles	39
18	Shot Silk	35
18	Signora	35
18	Violinista Costa	35
21	Opera	34
21	Cynthia Brooke	34
23	McGredy's Ivory	25
23	Barbara Richards	25

Table 5.—(Nurserymen, North)

Position	NAME	Number of Points
1	Ena Harkness	322
2	Peace	234
3	Spek's Yellow	224
4	McGredy's Yellow	208
5	Mrs. Sam McGredy	179
6	Crimson Glory...	174
7	Picture	159
8	Shot Silk	134
9	Lady Sylvia	130
10	Comtesse Vandal	120
11	The Doctor	106
12	McGredy's Sunset	103
13	President Herbert Hoover	99
14	Charles Gregory	79
15	Golden Melody	74
15	Phyllis Gold	74
15	Hector Deane	74
18	Lady Belper	64
19	Sutter's Gold	61
20	Etoile de Hollande	59
21	Signora	54
22	Fantasia	53
23	Flaming Sunset	51
24	Madame Butterfly	49

Table 6.—ROSES FOR GENERAL GARDEN CULTIVATION (North)

Position	Total No. of Points	Pointed by Amateurs	Pointed by Nurserymen	NAME	Date of Introduction	COLOUR
1	492	170	322	*†Ena Harkness	1946	Rich glowing red
2	408	174	234	†Peace	1947	Light yellow, edged pink
3	322	114	208	†McGredy's Yellow	1933	Pale Yellow
4	291	112	179	†Mrs. Sam McGredy	1929	Coppery orange, splashed red
5	269	110	159	†Picture	1932	Clear rose pink
6	260	86	174	*†Crimson Glory	1935	Deep velvety crimson
7	245	21	224	Spek's Yellow	1948	Golden yellow
8	178	72	106	*†The Doctor	1939	Bright silvery rose
9	174	54	120	Comtesse Vandal	1932	Reddish copper edged pale pink
10	169	39	130	*†Lady Sylvia	1927	Flesh pink, yellow base
10	169	35	134	*†Shot Silk...	1923	Orange rose shaded yellow
12	161	87	74	*Golden Melody	1939	Buff yellow
13	159	85	74	†Phyllis Gold	1934	Golden yellow
14	145	46	99	*†President Herbert Hoover ...	1930	Orange and red
15	136	77	59	*†Etoile de Hollande ...	1919	Bright dark red
16	124	21	103	†McGredy's Sunset	1937	Yellow flushed scarlet
17	100	51	49	*†Madame Butterfly	1920	Pink shaded apricot
18	93	14	79	*†Charles Gregory	1947	Rich vermilion shaded gold
19	92	18	74	*Hector Deane	1938	Brilliant salmon cerise
20	89	35	54	Signora	1936	Orange and flame red
21	78	14	64	Lady Belper	1948	Bronzy orange
22	69	35	34	†Violinista Costa...	1920	Scarlet shaded strawberry and gold
23	67	22	45	†Betty Uprichard	1921	Orange pink
24	61	42	19	*†Golden Dawn	1923	Pale lemon yellow

* The most highly fragrant varieties. † The most suitable for standards.

ROSES FOR GENERAL GARDEN CULTIVATION

Table 7.—(Amateurs, South)

Position	NAME	Number of Points
1	Peace	306
2	Ena Harkness	291
3	Crimson Glory	268
4	McGredy's Yellow	239
5	Spek's Yellow	193
6	Picture	170
7	Lady Sylvia	154
8	Mrs. Sam McGredy	146
9	Phyllis Gold	142
10	President Herbert Hoover	130
11	Golden Dawn	119
12	Madame Butterfly	103
13	Red Ensign	98
14	Etoile de Hollande	82
14	The Doctor	82
16	Shot Silk	76
16	Lady Belper	76
16	Violinista Costa	76
19	Golden Melody	69
20	McGredy's Sunset	60
21	Comtesse Vandal	56
22	Charlotte Armstrong	46
22	Karl Herbst	46
24	Mrs. H. Bowles	43

Table 8.—(Nurserymen, South)

Position	NAME	Number of Points
1	Peace	197
2	Ena Harkness	193
3	Spek's Yellow	181
4	Crimson Glory	163
5	Lady Sylvia	153
6	Picture	147
7	McGredy's Yellow	120
8	President Herbert Hoover	110
9	Madame Butterfly	89
10	Mrs. Sam McGredy	77
11	Shot Silk	69
12	The Doctor	67
13	Lady Belper	57
14	Golden Dawn	50
15	McGredy's Sunset	47
16	Violinista Costa	42
17	Betty Uprichard	39
18	Etoile de Hollande	38
19	Phyllis Gold	33
20	Flaming Sunset	32
21	Ellinor Le Grice	28
22	Golden Melody	27
23	Comtesse Vandal	26
24	Red Ensign	22

Table 9.—ROSES FOR GENERAL GARDEN CULTIVATION (South)

Position	Total No. of Points	Pointed by Amateurs	Pointed by Nurserymen	NAME	Date of Introduction	COLOUR
1	503	306	197	†Peace	1947	Golden yellow petals edged pink
2	484	291	193	*†Ena Harkness	1946	Scarlet crimson
3	431	268	163	*†Crimson Glory	1935	Deep velvety crimson
4	374	193	181	Spek's Yellow	1948	Golden yellow
5	359	239	120	†McGredy's Yellow	1933	Pale yellow
6	317	170	147	†Picture	1932	Clear rose pink
7	307	154	153	*†Lady Sylvia	1927	Flesh pink, yellow base
8	240	130	110	*†President Herbert Hoover ...	1930	Orange and red
9	223	146	77	†Mrs. Sam McGredy	1929	Coppery orange, splashed red
10	192	103	89	*†Madame Butterfly	1920	Pink shaded apricot
11	175	142	33	†Phyllis Gold	1934	Golden yellow
12	169	119	50	*†Golden Dawn	1923	Pale lemon yellow
13	149	82	67	*†The Doctor	1939	Bright silvery rose
14	145	76	69	*†Shot Silk	1923	Orange rose, shaded yellow
15	133	76	57	Lady Belper	1948	Bronzy orange
16	120	98	22	*Red Ensign	1947	Deep crimson
16	120	82	38	*†Etoile de Hollande	1919	Bright dark red
18	118	76	42	†Violinista Costa	1920	Scarlet shaded strawberry and gold
19	107	60	47	†McGredy's Sunset	1937	Yellow, flushed scarlet
20	96	69	27	*Golden Melody	1939	Buff yellow
21	82	56	26	Comtesse Vandal	1932	Reddish copper, edged pale pink
22	58	19	39	†Betty Uprichard	1921	Orange pink
23	52	34	18	Tally Ho	1949	Cerise buds, deep pink
24	48	16	32	Flaming Sunset	1947	Deep orange

* The most highly fragrant varieties. † The most suitable for standards.

ROSES SUITABLE FOR GARDEN PURPOSES

And which will also give large specimen blooms for exhibition

Table 10.—(Amateurs) Table 11.—(Nurserymen)

Position	NAME	Number of Points	Position	NAME	Number of Points
1	Peace	479	1	Peace	533
2	Ena Harkness	389	2	Ena Harkness	484
3	McGredy's Yellow	346	3	Crimson Glory	414
4	Crimson Glory	322	4	McGredy's Yellow	402
5	Phyllis Gold	319	5	The Doctor	349
6	The Doctor	315	6	McGredy's Ivory	257
7	Red Ensign	275	7	Golden Melody	255
8	Barbara Richards	273	8	Red Ensign	233
9	William Harvey	212	9	Barbara Richards	227
10	Golden Dawn	192	10	Mrs. Sam McGredy	219
11	McGredy's Ivory	190	11	Phyllis Gold	212
11	Glory of Rome	190	12	Glory of Rome	204
13	Directeur Guerin	173	13	Golden Dawn	194
14	Mrs. H. Bowles	172	14	William Harvey	188
15	Golden Melody	170	15	Comtesse Vandal	174
16	Dr. F. G. Chandler	144	16	Mrs. H. Bowles	173
17	Charlotte Armstrong	133	17	Dame Edith Helen	146
18	Mrs. Sam McGredy	132	18	Charlotte Armstrong	130
19	Comtesse Vandal	118	19	Lady Belper	114
20	Dame Edith Helen	117	20	Mrs. A. R. Barraclough	103
21	Mrs. A. R. Barraclough	100	21	Karl Herbst	99
22	Show Girl	94	22	Symphonie	97
23	Karl Herbst	93	23	Verschurens Pink	84
24	Sir Henry Segrave	90	24	Lal	78

Table 12.—GARDEN ROSES AND SPECIMEN BLOOMS

Position	Total No. of Points	Pointed by Amateurs	Pointed by Nurserymen	NAME	Date of Introduction	COLOUR
1	1,012	479	533	Peace	1947	Golden yellow, petals edged pink
2	875	389	484	Ena Harkness	1946	Scarlet crimson
3	748	346	402	McGredy's Yellow	1933	Pale yellow
4	736	322	414	Crimson Glory	1935	Deep velvety crimson
5	664	315	349	The Doctor	1939	Bright silvery rose
6	531	319	212	Phyllis Gold	1934	Golden yellow
7	508	275	233	Red Ensign	1947	Deep crimson
8	500	273	227	Barbara Richards	1930	Maize yellow, flushed rose
9	447	190	257	McGredy s Ivory	1939	Creamy white, shaded yellow
10	425	170	255	Golden Melody	1939	Buff yellow
11	400	212	188	William Harvey	1947	Dusky scarlet red
12	394	190	204	Glory of Rome	1937	Reddish pink
13	386	192	194	Golden Dawn	1923	Pale lemon yellow
14	351	132	219	Mrs. Sam McGredy	1929	Coppery orange, splashed red
15	345	172	173	Mrs. H. Bowles	1921	Glowing rose
16	292	118	174	Comtesse Vandal	1932	Reddish copper edged pale pink
17	263	117	146	Dame Edith Helen	1926	Pure glowing pink
17	263	133	130	Charlotte Armstrong	1950	Carmine shaded orange and pink
19	203	100	103	Mrs. A. R. Barraclough	1926	Carmine pink
20	192	173	19	Directeur Guerin	1937	Cream shaded gold
20	192	93	99	Karl Herbst	1950	Scarlet
22	191	144	47	Dr. F. G Chandler	1948	Velvety crimson
23	156	94	62	Show Girl	1950	Deep pink
24	134	90	44	Sir Henry Segrave	1932	Pale lemon yellow

WICHURAIANA CLIMBERS and WICHURAIANA RAMBLERS

These tables include only the wichuraiana climbers and ramblers. For the large flowered climbers see tables 16, 17 and 18.

Table 13.—(Amateurs) / Table 14.—(Nurserymen)

Position	NAME	Number of Points	Position	NAME	Number of Points
1	Albertine	263	1	Albertine	380
2	Paul's Scarlet	255	2	Paul's Scarlet	345
3	Chaplin's Pink	223	3	Chaplin's Pink	301
4	Crimson Conquest	212	4	Emily Gray	288
5	Emily Gray	192	5	American Pillar	240
6	American Pillar	185	6	Excelsa	235
7	Dr. Van Fleet	184	7	Crimson Conquest	220
8	Excelsa	166	8	The New Dawn	218
9	Easlea's Golden Rambler	146	9	Easlea's Golden Rambler	196
10	Alberic Barbier	134	10	Dr. Van Fleet	189
11	The New Dawn	133	11	Alberic Barbier	156
12	Francois Juranville	118	12	Francois Juranville	155
13	Dorothy Perkins	79	13	Dorothy Perkins	146
14	Sanders White	69	14	Mary Wallace	122
15	Minnehaha	68	15	Minnehaha	100
16	Mary Wallace	65	16	Sanders White	93
17	Thelma	58	17	Thelma	60
18	Lady Godiva	49	18	Blaze	49

Table 15.—WICH. CLIMBERS AND WICH. RAMBLERS

Position	Total No. of Points	Pointed by Amateurs	Pointed by Nurserymen	NAME	Date of Introduction	COLOUR
1	643	263	380	Albertine	1921	Coppery chamois passing to salmon
2	600	255	345	Paul's Scarlet	1916	Scarlet
3	524	223	301	Chaplin's Pink	1929	Warm pink
4	480	192	288	Emily Gray	1916	Golden yellow
5	432	212	220	Crimson Conquest	1931	Scarlet
6	425	185	240	American Pillar	1909	Clear rose, pink eye
7	401	166	235	Excelsa	1909	Bright rose crimson splashed red
8	373	184	189	Dr. Van Fleet	1910	Soft blush
9	351	133	218	The New Dawn	1930	Soft delicate pink
10	342	146	196	Easlea's Golden Rambler ...	1932	Golden yellow
11	290	134	156	Alberic Barbier	1900	Yellow bud changing to cream white
12	273	118	155	Francois Juranville	1906	Deep fawn pink
13	225	79	146	Dorothy Perkins	1901	Rose pink
14	187	65	122	Mary Wallace	1924	Clear rose pink
15	168	68	100	Minnehaha	1905	Deep pink
16	162	69	93	Sanders White	1912	White
17	118	58	60	Thelma	1927	Coral pink
18	86	37	49	Blaze	1932	Scarlet

LARGE FLOWERED CLIMBERS

Table 16.—(Amateurs) / Table 17.—(Nurserymen)

Position	NAME	Number of Points	Position	NAME	Number of Points
1	Lemon Pillar	181	1	Mermaid	237
2	Mermaid	151	2	Cl. Etoile de Hollande	205
3	Cl. Etoile de Hollande	130	3	Lemon Pillar	151
4	Cl. Madame Butterfly	111	3	Cl. Crimson Glory	151
5	Cl. Crimson Glory	109	5	Cl. Mrs. Sam McGredy	144
6	Cl. Shot Silk	91	6	Cl. Shot Silk	121
7	Cl. Mrs. Sam McGredy	86	7	Cl. Golden Dawn	102
8	Allen Chandler	83	8	Cl. Madame Butterfly	95
9	Cl. Mme. Caroline Testout	64	9	Cl. Madame E. Herriot	89
10	Cl. Golden Dawn	59	10	Madame G. Staechelin	71
11	Cl. Madame E. Herriot	43	11	Allen Chandler	65
12	Madame G. Staechelin	28	12	Guinee	53

Table 18.—LARGE FLOWERED CLIMBERS AND SPORTS

Position	Total No. of Points	Pointed by Amateurs	Pointed by Nurserymen	NAME	Date of Introduction	COLOUR
1	388	151	237	Mermaid	1917	Pale sulphur yellow
2	335	130	205	Cl. Etoile de Hollande	1932	Bright dark red
3	332	181	151	Lemon Pillar	1915	Sulphur yellow
4	260	109	151	Cl. Crimson Glory	1946	Deep velvety crimson
5	230	86	144	Cl. Mrs. Sam McGredy	1937	Coppery orange flushed scarlet
6	212	91	121	Cl. Shot Silk	1937	Cerise, shaded orange salmon
7	206	111	95	Cl. Madame Butterfly	1925	Pink shaded apricot
8	161	59	102	Cl. Golden Dawn	1934	Pale lemon yellow
9	148	83	65	Allen Chandler	1924	Vivid scarlet
10	132	43	89	Cl. Madame E. Herriot	1921	Coral red shaded yellow
11	114	64	50	Cl. Mme. Caroline Testout ...	1902	Bright warm pink
12	99	28	71	Madame G. Staechelin	1927	Pale coral shaded pink

DWARF POLYANTHA ROSES

Table 19.—(Amateurs)

Position	NAME	Number of Points
1	Paul Crampel	160
2	Cameo	127
3	Coral Cluster	114
4	Golden Salmon Superior	93
5	Little Dorritt	88
6	Gloria Mundi...	82
7	Ellen Poulsen	73
8	Gloire du Midi	72
9	Edith Cavell	66
10	Ideal	42
11	Willy den Ouden	27
12	Eblouissant	26

Table 20.—(Nurserymen)

Position	NAME	Number of Points
1	Paul Crampel	258
2	Cameo	190
3	Golden Salmon Superior	175
4	Little Dorritt	156
5	Ellen Poulsen	139
6	Coral Cluster	114
7	Edith Cavell	99
8	Ideal	84
9	Gloria Mundi	77
10	Gloire du Midi	57
11	Orleans Rose	53
12	Yvonne Rabier	34

Table 21.—DWARF POLYANTHA ROSES

Position	Total No. of Points	Pointed by Amateurs	Pointed by Nurserymen	NAME	Date of Introduction	COLOUR
1	418	160	258	Paul Crampel	1930	Deep orange red
2	317	127	190	Cameo	1932	Flesh pink
3	268	93	175	Golden Salmon Superior ...	1926	Vivid golden salmon
4	244	88	156	Little Dorritt	1930	Coral salmon
5	228	114	114	Coral Cluster	1920	Pale coral pink
6	212	73	139	Ellen Poulsen	1921	Bright cherry red
7	165	66	99	Edith Cavell	1917	Bright cherry crimson, white eye
8	159	82	77	Gloria Mundi	1929	Glowing orange
9	129	72	57	Gloire du Midi	1932	Brilliant orange scarlet
10	126	42	84	Ideal	1921	Dark scarlet
11	71	18	53	Orleans Rose	1909	Vivid rosy crimson, white centre
12	53	27	26	Willy den Ouden	1938	Vivid salmon

FLORIBUNDA ROSES
Hybrid Polyantha

Table 22.—(Amateurs)

Position	NAME	Number of Points
1	Frensham	364
2	Fashion	295
3	Orange Triumph (hyb. mosc.) ..	249
3	Dainty Maid	249
5	Donald Prior	212
6	Karen Poulsen	175
7	Dusky Maiden	161
8	Alain	151
9	Else Poulsen	126
10	De Ruiters Herald (hyb. mosc.) ...	97
11	Anne Poulsen	91
12	Goldilocks	87
13	Salmon Spray	84
14	Van Nes	79
14	Poulsen's Pink	79
16	Commonwealth	77
17	Border Queen	76
18	Betty Prior	72

Table 23.—(Nurserymen)

Position	NAME	Number of Points
1	Frensham	372
2	Fashion	365
3	Orange Triumph (hyb. mosc.) ...	273
4	Donald Prior	226
5	Alain	214
6	Dainty Maid	202
7	Goldilocks	198
8	Karen Poulsen	144
9	Anne Poulsen	136
10	De Ruiters Herald (hyb. mosc.)	128
11	Poulsen's Bedder	124
12	Dusky Maiden	105
13	Border Queen	96
14	Commonwealth	92
15	Else Poulsen	88
16	Salmon Spray	55
17	Pinocchio	54
18	Vogue	53

Table 24.—FLORIBUNDA ROSES
Hybrid Polyantha

Position	Total No. of Points	Pointed by Amateurs	Pointed by Nurserymen	NAME	Date of Introduction	COLOUR
1	736	364	372	Frensham	1946	Deep scarlet
2	660	295	365	Fashion	1949	Coral Peach
3	522	249	273	Orange Triumph (hyb. mosc.) ...	1938	Orange scarlet
4	451	249	202	Dainty Maid	1938	Carmine, shaded pink
5	438	212	226	Donald Prior	1934	Scarlet flush pink
6	365	151	214	Alain	1948	Bright carmine red
7	319	175	144	Karen Poulsen	1933	Intense scarlet
8	285	87	198	Goldilocks	1949	Deep yellow
9	266	161	105	Dusky Maiden	1946	Rich crimson
10	227	91	136	Anne Poulsen	1935	Crimson red
11	225	97	128	De Ruiters Herald (hyb. mosc.)	1948	Orange scarlet
12	214	126	88	Else Poulsen	1924	Bright rose pink
13	172	76	96	Border Queen		Salmon pink to orange red
14	169	77	92	Commonwealth	1948	Cerise scarlet
15	143	19	124	Poulsen's Bedder	1949	Rosy pink
16	139	84	55	Salmon Spray	1935	Salmon pink shaded carmine
17	122	79	43	Poulsen's Pink	1939	Pink shaded gold
18	119	72	47	Betty Prior	1934	Pale pink, white centre

AUDIT OF NEWER ROSES

These tables include all Roses introduced in this country since 1947.

Table 25.—(Amateurs)

Position	NAME	Number of Points
1	Karl Herbst	224
2	Spek's Yellow	213
3	Fashion	200
4	Charlotte Armstrong	169
5	Eden Rose	167
6	Symphonie	159
6	Lady Belper	159
8	Grand'mere Jenny	130
9	Sutter's Gold	126
10	Verschurens Pink	125
11	Gordon Eddie	114
12	Show Girl	112
13	Independence	90
14	Opera	87
15	Dorothy Anderson	86
16	Gay Crusader...	82
17	Dr. Debat	69
18	Charles Mallerin	65

Table 26.—(Nurserymen)

Position	NAME	Number of Points
1	Fashion	286
2	Spek's Yellow	227
3	Sutter's Gold	197
4	Lady Belper	190
5	Independence	182
6	Grand'mere Jenny	168
7	Monique	161
8	Eden Rose	120
9	Opera	117
10	Symphonie	111
11	Verschurens Pink	93
12	Charlotte Armstrong	92
13	Marcel Gret	87
14	Charles Mallerin	83
15	Karl Herbst	82
16	Fantasia	78
17	Flaming Sunset	74
18	Dr. Debat	72

Table 27.—AUDIT OF NEWER ROSES

Position	Total No. of Points	Pointed by Amateurs	Pointed by Nurserymen	NAME	Date of Introduction	COLOUR
1	486	200	286	Fashion Hyb. Poly.	1949	Coral peach
2	440	213	227	Spek's Yellow H.T.	1948	Golden yellow
3	349	159	190	Lady Belper, H.T.	1948	Bronzy orange
4	323	126	197	Sutter's Gold, H.T.	1950	Yellow pink
5	306	224	82	Karl Herbst, H.T....	1950	Scarlet
6	298	130	168	Grand'mere Jenny, H.T. ...	1950	Peach, outer petals shaded pink
7	287	167	120	Eden Rose	1950	Bright madder pink
8	272	90	182	Independence, H.T.	1950	Orange scarlet
9	270	159	111	Symphonie, H.T.	1949	Carmine
10	261	169	92	Charlotte Armstrong, H.T. ...	1949	Carmine, shaded orange pink
11	218	125	93	Verschurens Pink, H.T.	1949	Rose pink, deep shadings
12	204	87	117	Opera, H.T.	1950	Dark carmine, coppery shade reverse background
13	201	40	161	Monique	1949	Bright pink, salmon pink
14	180	114	66	Gordon Eddie	1950	Buff orange
15	148	65	83	Charles Mallerin, H.T.	1948	Dark crimson
16	141	69	72	Dr. Debat	1948	Soft pink, gold at base
17	137	112	25	Show Girl	1950	Deep pink
18	133	82	51	Gay Crusader	1948	Outside deep yellow, inner orange and scarlet

Table 28.—SHRUB ROSES

An increasing number of Rose growers are looking for "no trouble" shrubs for their mixed borders and for backgrounds or hedges. This new table will help to fill that demand.

Position	Total No. of Points	Pointed by Amateurs	Pointed by Nurserymen	NAME	COLOUR	Height in feet
1	182	85	97	*†R. moyesii	Dusky scarlet, brilliant red heps	8—10
2	136	76	60	Penelope (hyb. mosc.)	Pink shaded salmon	5
3	129	72	50	*R. hugonis	Yellow	7
4	91	18	73	Cornelia (hyb. mosc.)	Apricot flushed pink	5—6
5	85	44	41	Conrad F. Meyer (hyb. rug.) ...	Silvery pink	5—6
6	80	16	64	Grandmaster (hyb. mosc.) ...	Buff pink	4—6
7	70	46	24	Nevada (hyb. moyesii)	Pale flesh	6—7
8	66	37	29	Bonn (hyb. mosc.)	Bright red	5—6
9	64	21	43	Elmshorn (hyb. mosc.)	Bright crimson	5
10	62	23	39	Felicia (hyb. mosc.)	Salmon pink shaded yellow ...	6
11	55	18	37	Schneezwerg (hyb. rug.) ...	White	4—5
12	44	24	20	*R. willmottiae	Mauve pink	8—9

*Summer flowering only.
† Summer flowering with autumn heps.

THE HARROW HORTICULTURAL AND ROSE SOCIETY CENTENARY, 1853—1953

The Harrow Horticultural and Rose Society this year celebrates its Centenary. The Society was orginally founded by a few residents on Harrow Hill and was known as the Harrow Rose Society, due no doubt to Roses growing to such perfection on our heavy clay soil. We often wonder whether the theory that Roses thrive on clay soil emanated from this Society.

We have always encouraged the growing of Roses among our members, this flower being the main attraction at our Summer Show when we average twenty classes. It is with pleasure that we record among our past members the late Mr. Chas. H. Rigg and the late Dr. A. H. Williams, both past Presidents of the National Rose Society, and it was during his membership with us that Dr. Williams raised that well-known climbing Rose, Emily Gray. For the last three years we have competed in the Affiliated Societies Class at the National Show, being successful in winning the Franklin Dennison Memorial Cup on two occasions and runner-up on the third.

By kind permission of Kodak, Ltd., our Summer Show this year will be held in the Company's Concert Hall at Wealdstone on July the 4th and 5th.

E. L. B.

Your garden, whether small or large,
deserves the best

STEDMAN'S ROSES

ADD DISTINCTION TO EVERY GARDEN

Catalogue of Bushes, Climbers,
Musks, Species and Old Varieties
available Post Free on request.

E. W. STEDMAN, LTD.

The Rose Gardens

LONGTHORPE - PETERBOROUGH